BECO[ ] A RICHER WRITER

Shift Your Writing Career Into High Gear

Gene Perret

Jester Press
Westlake Village, CA

Library of Congress Cataloging-in-Publication Data

Perret, Gene.
[Shift your writing career into high gear]
Become a richer writer: shift your writing
career into high gear/by Gene Perret
p. cm.
Originally published under the title:
Shift your writing career into high gear. 1993.
1. Authorship.   2. Authorship - Marketing.
I. Title.   II. Title: Shift your writing career into high gear.
PN147.P44 1996
808'.02 - dc20

ISBN: 1-888688-01-7

Edited by Anita Buck
Cover Design by Heidi Frieder

Printed and bound in the United States of America

Published by Jester Press
30941 W. Agoura Rd. #228
Westlake Village, CA 91361

ABOUT THE AUTHOR

Award-winning comedy writer Gene Perret has enjoyed a variety of careers ranging from engineer, writer and producer, to head writer, author, publisher, and prize-winning public speaker. One of the roles he values most has been teaching writing through books, seminars, an international newsletter in its eleventh year, his annual comedy-writing workshops, and a humor-writing course at Northern Arizona University.

A three-time Emmy winner, Perret also holds a Writers Guild Award, and was voted the International Platform Association's "Outstanding Discovery in the Field of Humor."

Perret has written for "Laugh-In," "The Carol Burnett Show," "The New Bill Cosby Show," "Welcome Back, Kotter," "Three's Company" and "The Tim Conway Show." For more than twenty years, he has written for Bob Hope's TV specials and personal appearances and has been Hope's head writer for the past five years. Perret has written for Phyllis Diller, Slappy White, and many of the nation's favorite entertainers.

Among his ten books are how-to volumes on writing comedy, public speaking, and adult and juvenile collections of humor. For nine years Perret has produced, hosted and led seminars for participants of his *Round Table* newsletter. Several former students now write and produce TV sitcoms, and work full-time for such entertainers as Bob Hope and Jay Leno.

*This book
is dedicated to
my own
next generation
of writers*

TABLE OF CONTENTS

INTRODUCTION

I was a fussy eater as a youngster. Whenever I balked at a new recipe or resisted a vegetable that appeared less than appetizing, my mom would say, "Eat it; it's good for what ails you."

I might paraphrase Mom's saying in offering this book to writers: "Read it; it's good for what ails you." More accurately, it's good for what ails your writing career.

Let's face it: Beginning writer, journeyman, superstar—we're all dissatisfied with our progress at one time or another. It should be moving faster, further or in a different direction.

Writing is a profession that demands passion. If we didn't have a devotion to our craft that bordered on the fanatical, we wouldn't do what we do. We wouldn't do it for very long, anyway. It's that writer's zeal that urges us to speed forward. And it's that same fervor that distresses us when our progress stops, or even slows.

However, our writing proficiency and our success in selling vary. They depend on our education—formal and informal— our experience, the marketplace and other intangibles. There are plateaus that we must reach and progress through in our climb toward the kind of work and sales we want. Some of these plateaus are learning experiences that will help our writing mature. Some are just plain obstacles.

Then there are creative and emotional highs and lows that affect us. One day we're inspired with a magnificent story, the next day we can't find the words to convert it to the typewritten page. One day we write an eloquent query letter, the next day the editor rejects the premise. One day we complete the final chapter of our Great American Novel, the next day Cousin Martha reads the manuscript and finds the characters weak and the story line contrived.

There are peaks and valleys in a writing career, which most writers actually prefer. It's not monotonous, like the repetitious, nine-to-five, do-today-the-same-as-you-did-yesterday type of workday. It's an adventure, it's excitement. Yes, most writers I know prefer the peaks and valleys.

Except for the valleys.

The valleys, even when they serve a purpose—and many of them do—still are frustrating. They slow us down when we'd much rather get where we want to be.

I wrote for Phyllis Diller for almost a year before I finally met her in person. She gave my writing a tremendous compliment, which naturally pleased me. However, it also puzzled me. I said, "Phyllis, if my writing's that good, how come I'm not in Hollywood?"

She said, "Gene, you're not ready yet."

Phyllis was right. Like all writers, I wanted to race to glory. I wanted to get there whether I had the seasoning or not. I wanted to skip the minor leagues and rush right into the majors. But I wasn't ready.

Throughout your writing adventure, you'll have ups and downs, peaks and valleys, spurts and stalls. Your highs will be glorious and your lows will be difficult. Ghastly, sometimes. The downs, valleys, stalls—whatever you choose to call them—happen to all of us. I guarantee that those writers who have three books on the bestseller list would rather have four or five. It's part of the passion in the writer's heart.

The premise of this book is that when you hit the valleys—and you will, for they're the cold, hard, realistic facts of the writing business—they might slow down your career temporarily, but they needn't dampen your enthusiasm. You can, in fact, work through those periods—and be a better writer for having done so.

You can effectively use those times to add momentum to your writing career, so that when you emerge from the slowdown, you'll emerge with added acceleration. You'll shift your writing career into high gear.

You'll endure and survive the valleys, the way I had to swallow some of those unidentifiable vegetables that Mom piled on my plate. And again I paraphrase my mom's advice: "Read it; it's good for what ails you."

PART I

LOOK TO YOURSELF

"There is only one success —
to be able to spend
your life in your own way."

CHRISTOPHER MARLEY

CHAPTER 1

IT'S YOUR CAREER

A mother brought her youngster for his first day at school. She advised the teacher, "Julius is a sensitive child. If he's naughty, slap the child next to him. That'll scare him into being good."

That's a silly joke, but many of us writers (and other people, too) subscribe to the same philosophy as Julius's mother. Often we want the Fates to slap the writer next to us when we're at fault.

This is your writing career. You have to take control of it. It doesn't belong to the other writers you know, nor to the editors, publishers or producers that you deal with. It's yours. Like little Julius, you must take the occasional rap on the knuckles. You must assume the responsibility, endure the setbacks—and enjoy the rewards.

Once you accept that philosophy—that you're in control, that you're the one doing the driving—you can begin to shift your career into high gear. You can now determine where you're going and what your success will be.

I realize that sounds a bit simplistic, but it's true. At least, it's true to the extent that you have the potential to go where you want and do what you want. It's true to the extent, too, that you have a better chance of going where you want and doing what you want than you have of someone getting you there and doing it for you.

Some of us reject rags-to-riches stories as fairy tales that only happen in novels and are recounted in motivational speeches.

Not true; they do happen. In my own experience, I've known and worked side by side with people who had money and career problems. Then — *bang!* — it happened. They got their break; they found their niche. Now they're among the wealthiest and most powerful people in Hollywood.

Knowing these people, though, I know that they worked for their success. They did what they had to do. They took charge. They were in control.

Napoleon Hill, who wrote *Think and Grow Rich*, one of the best and most valid self-help books of all time, said, "Whatever the mind of man can conceive and believe, it can achieve." I interpret that as meaning, "If you have a goal you think might be possible, it is possible." At the very least, you can work toward its attainment.

But you have to be in control; you have to take charge. To be in control, you must:

1. Decide on *your own* goal.
2. Be willing to pay the price for that goal.
3. Take steps to achieve it.
4. Do the work *yourself.*

DECIDE ON *YOUR OWN* GOAL

Obviously, if you want to get somewhere, you must have some idea of where you're going. If you get in your car and open a road map, you must have a destination in mind. So you, the writer, should have some objective in mind. It might be a detailed list of your long- and short-term goals, complete with definite dates for their accomplishment; or it can be simply a vague, general notion. That's up to you. But know where you're headed.

Equally important, though, is that this destination should be your own. It can't be a goal your parents or your spouse selected for you. It can't be one that society's traditional values have handed to you. It must not be one that your agent chooses for you. It has to be *your* choice, *your* desire, *your* goal.

Goals are neither good nor bad, worthy nor unworthy; they simply *are*. An accomplishment that's worthwhile for one person might be a waste of time for another.

You have to genuinely want, wish and dream for something before it becomes a worthwhile goal. If it's *your* goal, it's worth pursuing.

BE WILLING TO PAY THE PRICE FOR YOUR GOAL

Understand, though, that your goal is more than a dream or a wish; it's a responsibility. It has a price tag. Suppose, for example, that I could magically make you the president of General Motors, with all of its perks. It seems pleasant enough. It's high-paying. You get a nice office. You travel first-class everywhere and even have a limo pick you up at the airport. It's pretty soft, right?

But being president of General Motors is more than that. It's keeping your corporation competitive. It's overseeing the day-to-day operations of this massive company. It's being a tough, hard-nosed businessperson. It's being competent. Unless you can do all those things, you'll have more heartaches than thrills as the president of General Motors.

However, if you have a sincere desire for a particular goal and are willing to pay the price for its attainment, then you are in control.

TAKE THE STEPS TO ACHIEVE IT

When you formulate a goal and take control of achieving it, you take responsibility for many other factors, too. To be a successful writer, you must assume responsibility for your education, research, production, marketing, PR, advertising, communication, sales — in short, everything. You can't decide to win the Pulitzer Prize for Drama and then sit back and wait for the committee to notify you. If you're not good enough to qualify for the Pulitzer yet, it's not the prize committee's fault; it's your fault.

Being in control doesn't automatically mean getting what you want. It means having the *potential* to get what you want. Wanting something badly will rarely get it for you. Wanting something badly enough to do whatever's required to get it, though, often will.

Suppose, for example, you want to become a regular contributor to *Reader's Digest*. That's a commendable goal because the periodical is not only high paying, but prestigious. The *Digest's* editors demand thorough research and exceptional writing. Can you become one of their regulars? Do you have the potential to do it? Sure you do, but you have some work to do.

Read the magazine thoroughly, to know which type of articles it prints and which writing style it prefers. Become familiar with its classifications of articles and decide which ones you can write. Inspirational articles? Personality profiles? Humor? Articles about dramatic events in the news? Health? Economics?

You must determine what you have to offer the *Digest*. Can you write an authoritative article on a new surgical procedure? Can you do a personality piece about a celebrity? Can you write a humorous article?

Find out which types of articles the magazine is most inclined to purchase from first-time authors. Then develop a few ideas to submit for the editor's consideration, and write a proposal, or at least a query letter.

The point of all this is that you're actively pursuing your goal, not merely wishing it. You're taking charge. If there are steps to be taken, you're taking them.

If you do all this groundwork and then honestly decide you're not yet ready for the *Digest*, that's okay. That's progress. That's recognizing that you have more work to do. That's taking charge of your own career.

However, if you just assume that *Reader's Digest* wouldn't be interested in you or your writing, that's baloney. That's putting someone else in charge.

This is your career, not *Reader's Digest's*.

YOU MUST DO THE WORK

You must do the work to get where you want to go. Not I; not the editors at *Reader's Digest*; not a friend who has a friend who knows someone who has a relative who works at *Reader's Digest*. You have to do it.

In my work with aspiring writers, I'm often surprised at how many people want success without any effort. Well, they know some effort has to be expended, but they want others to expend it. I've had people in writing classes who never completed one assignment, never did any of the suggested homework. Then in their critique of the class they complained that they didn't learn anything. I've taught people who wanted to skim over the how-to classes, who ignored the recommendations for their writing improvement. They just wanted to get to the part where they sell their work and land a high-paying staff position. I've had students who wanted me to take their writing and present it, with an endorsement, to one of my clients. They expected me to do their marketing for them.

I've also watched aspiring writers improve and progress. Some of them have staff jobs in Hollywood now. They're the ones who did the work and took some risks on their own. They listened, learned and progressed. They took whatever advice was offered and analyzed it, researched it, acted on it, and did all the work themselves. They took the responsibility; they got the rewards.

Another reason you want to be in control is that you're the most powerful benefactor you've got in the writing profession. Other people—producers, editors, publishers, agents—can't really do much for you. Why? For several reasons.

Others Are Too Busy

Editors, whether we want to admit it or not, have their own sequence of problems to face each day. They have budgetary problems, scheduling problems, personnel problems, and personality problems that you can't even begin to imagine. They have an unreasonable boss who expects them to do twelve hours of work in an eight-hour day. They have incompetent workers who do four hours of work in that same eight-hour day (and expect a raise for doing it). They have writers who are late with their assignments, assistant editors who call in sick, and production assistants who lose the important files at the critical times.

It's not easy preparing a magazine for publication. Editors certainly don't have time to act as your spiritual writing guide, too. They have too many of their own worries to devote part of their day to worrying for you, also.

Others Are Unreliable

Other writers will graciously offer to read your manuscripts and offer incisive critiques. You'll never hear from them again. Agents will guarantee that they can take your writing and build a profitable career for you within months. Soon they'll be ducking your telephone calls. Editors will promise to get back to you within four weeks. After four months you'll have to write and remind them that they're a tad late.

Again, these aren't complaints or sour grapes; they're facts of the writing life. You can't force editors to read your queries or proposals. You can't extort a reply from them. You can't hurry them when they won't be hurried. You simply can't depend on others. So don't. Depend on yourself.

Others Have No Stake in Your Career

Editors may want to publish your book or print your article, but they don't really care whether you reach your goals as a writer.

Oh sure, you'll meet many fine people in the writing profession. You'll meet editors who do care about your development. You'll be blessed with agents who are concerned not only about your work but about you. Cherish these people and be good to them. Admit, though, that no one cares as much about your writing as you do. So, once again, it's your career; you take charge of it.

CHAPTER 2

REDEFINE YOUR ATTITUDES

Every parent has experienced some variation of this vacation scene: You load the car with luggage, checking as you do that you have all that you need. You cram, rearrange, force packages into spaces that they really don't fit into. Then you advise — no, you order — the children to visit the bathroom before leaving the house. You check that everything that should be turned off is turned off, everything that should be locked is locked.

You herd the youngsters into the car, then realize that they all want the same seat. You must assign seating over their protestations, with the promise that after so many miles they will get to change seats. Everyone will be happy during this trip because it is the family fun vacation.

Finally, you settle into the front seat and issue a stern warning to the children that you will not tolerate any teasing, fighting, screaming or excessive noise — especially no singing of long, irritating, repetitive songs. This vacation is meant to be fun and it will be fun whether they like it or not.

Finally, the car pulls away. After about six minutes of traveling time one of the children asks, "Are we there yet?"

Children are champions of instant gratification. They want their satisfaction immediately, unsullied by planning, preparation or responsibility of any kind. Writers, though, should know better. Every destination implies a journey. Each goal requires a struggle. A purchase suggests a price.

Not accepting this can cause attitude problems. It does with the kids on the trip. They want to go on vacation, but they don't want to sit as prisoners in the car during the long trip. So the bottom lips come out and they sulk. Or they insult the sibling sitting next to them, who in turn clobbers them over the head with a toy. Or they start a fight more to annoy their parents than to settle any dispute among themselves.

Writers, too, can have attitude problems on their journey to wherever they want to go. Those attitudes can affect performance. If you're depressed, your work is depressed. If you're frustrated, your output falters.

The mind influences the body. If you go on a cruise and people suggest that you look a little pale, a bit washed out, somewhat "green around the gills," by the end of the day you'll be in your cabin feeling queasy or downright seasick. People or circumstances suggest, you accept, and the body believes.

Your attitude also can influence your enthusiasm. Would you try to open a jammed window if someone told you that the window was welded closed? Would you pack a bag of goodies, load the kids in the car, and drive to the stadium if a news broadcaster told you that today's game was postponed? Of course not.

Would you keep trying to break into television writing if you honestly believed that television producers do not allow newcomers into the circle? Would you agonize over plot structure, character development and crisp dialogue if you were convinced that publishers will not buy first novels?

Your attitude can destroy your productivity, your incentive.

Following are a few of the troublesome attitudes to be wary of. The first is similar to that of the youngsters on that vacation trip.

"I WANT IT NOW"

Businesspeople tell me that most new businesses fail because they're underfunded. They don't have enough capital to sustain them throughout the start-up period or to ease them over the first few unexpected setbacks. Inexperienced entrepreneurs envision the huge profits but ignore the considerable expenses.

Everything has a price tag, including success. That's why well-advised entrepreneurs begin with a comprehensive business plan. How much will I need? Which pitfalls might I encounter? Where is the break-even point? How much profit can I expect? Establishing a successful, self-sustaining business requires time, effort, planning, perseverance, patience and maybe a touch of luck.

Writing is a business, too. Aspiring authors—and those anxious to move to the next plateau—require a business plan. Perhaps not as formal as the entrepreneur's, but just as realistic and objective. The writer must know, if not on paper, at least in his own mind what the investment is. How long will it take? How much trouble will it be?

All growth is gradual. But "gradual" doesn't mean slow; it simply means that it progresses on a step-by-step basis. Even so-called overnight success does. Authors of bestselling first novels, like Joseph Wambaugh and Jean Auel, had to outline their novels, research them, schedule their writing time, write and rewrite chapters and paragraphs, query publishers, pursue agents, negotiate contracts, and wait the agonizing months between the delivery of the manuscript and the publication of the book. It wasn't always easy, but it was necessary.

Expecting to shortcut too much of this—or any other process, for that matter—and not being able to, is frustrating. It's depressing and demoralizing. It's counterproductive and it's childish. It's wanting to get there as soon as you get in the car. Just as the kids' impatience disrupted the drive, so a writer's unreasonable restlessness can hamper career growth.

Welcome your success in bits and pieces. Accept your progress in plateaus. Recognize that certain steps take time. If you mail a manuscript today, you won't receive your reply tomorrow.

Each time I've sold a book, the moment of sale is truly gratifying. The publisher calls and says, "You have a go-ahead." It's glorious. I have a contract. I have a check to cash. However, I also have a book to write. That last part can seem overwhelming. I now have to convert a twelve-page outline, which often is a lot of "blue sky" and fluff, to 90,000 correctly spelled, properly punctuated, coherent words. It borders on the impossible.

I break the task into mathematical, bite-sized chunks. I have six months to complete 90,000 words. That amounts to a 15,000-word quota each month. Divide that again by four and I get a weekly assignment of 3,750 words. That works out to a daily requirement of only 750 words, with two days off for the weekends.

Now the project is workable. It's possible. We can all do the same thing with a writing goal: achieve it with patience, once we realize that we must approach it point by point, step by step.

"AND I WANT TO BE PAID FOR IT"

None of us wants to be underpaid, yet most of us feel we are. There are exceptions, like the man who was being considered for a new job. He asked what his salary would be and the personnel manager said, "We'll pay you whatever you're worth." The guy turned that offer down. He said, "Hell, I'm making more than that now."

Most of us don't have that kind of honesty, though. Look at the baseball player who makes headlines as the highest-paid player in major league history. Then, a few months into his record-breaking contract, he starts whining and wants to renegotiate his salary because some other player has signed for more money.

There's nothing wrong with any athlete, actor or author earning as much as she can. However, there might be something wrong with harboring resentment, like the man in the first story, over being paid what we're worth.

All of us read about the huge salaries some people command. We know that some popular writers make a lot of money from their books. They get hefty advances and large advertising and promotion budgets, along with many pleasant perks. You know that you're as good a writer, or better, than they are. So why don't you command those ridiculous figures? Because you haven't earned them—yet.

You'll command a large salary when you've proven your ability and your sales potential, and not until then. It can be demoralizing to think that you're not being paid what you deserve, but only if you permit it to be. Only if your attitude convinces you that you're being financially abused.

The other side of this coin is to use the elusive financial reward as an incentive. Keep your writing quality up. Keep pushing for your sales to improve. Eventually, you'll get the hit that will enable you to dictate the terms of your next contract. That's when you'll get your rewards.

"DON'T TELL ME IT CAN'T BE DONE, BECAUSE I'M GOING TO DO IT"

When I worked in industry, we used to kid about a guy who was so foolhardy and so dumb that you could get him to do almost anything. All you had to do was goad him into some imbecilic stunt or, better yet, bet him. We used to spread the apocryphal story that he once lost a bet that he could jump across a well in two jumps.

There are certain things that can't be done. When I was a youngster, my high-school-aged brother argued with me that it was impossible to draw a square circle. I spent hours with a pad and pencil trying to devise some way of drawing a figure that might somehow be considered a square circle. Eventually, after some weird designs, I abandoned the pursuit.

The square circle obviously is impossible, except to a hardheaded grade schooler, because it's a contradiction in terms. Some impossibilities are not nearly so apparent, but they're just as real. Yet many of us hard-headed writers insist on trying them. We spend entire careers, or a good part of our writing apprenticeships, trying to jump across a literary well in two jumps.

Let me give you an example. Breaking into television writing by creating a pilot is a practical impossibility. It's not exactly a square circle, but it's effectively about as close as you can come. And I'm not talking about established writers in other fields. A recognized short-story writer might be able to convince a network that he has a workable pilot idea, and the network might take a chance with it. A novelist or a screenwriter with established credits might begin a television career with a pilot. But an out-and-out writing novice has virtually no chance.

Here's why: Pilots are costly. Networks and producers are reluctant to release large amounts of money to untried talent. Also, it's hard to judge the merit of a pilot based on the presentation alone. It's the execution of the idea that breathes marketability into the project. Again, the networks and producers trust the execution to proven veterans rather than novices.

Those are the cold, hard facts of television reality. Yet, many beginning writers still will say, "I've got a great idea for a new pilot. Who can I take it to?" In effect, they're saying, "Take me to a well. I think I can get across it in two jumps."

Can a newcomer, then, ever sell a pilot? Certainly. How? By establishing some credentials. By writing episodes for various shows. Write a "Star Trek: The Next Generation" script; write a "Doogie Howser, M.D." episode. Write a movie or a novel. Build a writing reputation that the network executives can trust. *Then* sell the pilot.

There is a difference between impossibility and improbability. For many years, running a four-minute mile was considered impossible. Then Roger Bannister broke that barrier. Shortly thereafter, everyone was breaking it. Today, any world-class distance runner must run a less-than-four-minute mile to be a real Olympic threat.

Anyone who has achieved any sort of success has gone against the odds. They've all had someone at some time tell them that they couldn't do it, but they did it. That's persistence, not folly.

But how do you tell the difference? One way is to consider the source. Who's telling you that your goal is unattainable? Is it your mom? Aunt Mabel? Your pal Gordy? Well, they're nice people, but they might not know what they're talking about. They probably don't know as much about it as you do.

However, if the professionals are telling you, perhaps you should pay attention. And I don't mean just one or two professionals. That might be envy or inverted boasting. "You'll never be as good as I am because you're just a mere mortal. Give up the attempt and stick with your day job." But if every book you read, every seminar you attend, every responsible individual you talk to offers the same caution, it probably has merit.

Try to adopt an attitude of reality—cold, hard-nosed reality. Look pragmatically at what you're trying to accomplish. If it seems impossible and you still want to pursue it, at least pursue it as an avocation. Devote some of your precious writing time to a more traditional avenue to success. You can try to sell a pilot while you write short stories, novels, screenplays, teleplays or children's books at the same time. If you must try to jump across the well in two jumps, have a net under you.

"I'M TOO TALENTED TO BE BOUND BY RULES"

Sometimes in my speaking engagements I tell stories about a man who was assigned to pick me up at the airport and drive me to the hotel. He zoomed along the highway at frightening speeds. When we approached a red light he raced right through it, without even slowing down.

I said, "That was a red light, you know."

He said, "I know, but my brother taught me to drive and he never stops for red lights."

Then we came to a stop sign, and he never touched the brake.

I said, "You're supposed to stop for those."

He said, "My brother taught me to drive and he doesn't stop for stop signs, either."

We came to another red light and again, the guy zipped through it without even slowing down. I knew the reason so I didn't bother to ask—his brother taught him to drive, and his brother always goes through red lights.

Then we came to a green light, and my driver slammed on the brakes.

I said, "That was a green light. Why'd you stop for that?"

He said, "My brother might be coming."

I tell that story just to get a laugh, but there's a useful message embedded in there, too. Even when you don't obey the rules, you must obey *some* rules. If you insist on barreling through red lights, you must be careful of the green ones.

Writing has definite rules of spelling, grammar and structure. Every publisher develops guidelines of content and style. You're welcome to break or bend these rules. Or you can totally ignore them, if you like. That's the freedom of art as opposed to science. However, risk is involved. You're going in the face of the traditionalists, and many experienced writers find old habits hard to break and established beliefs difficult to surrender. I was raised to believe that turning the hands of a clock counterclockwise was unwise. Today I question that belief, but just to be on the safe side, I always turn the hands clockwise. If I don't will the clock break or explode? I don't know, and I'll never find out.

That's the way some editors tenaciously hang onto their writing precepts. You can disregard them, but you must realize that doing so could slow your progress.

"I HAVE NOTHING TO LEARN"

Those who think they know all there is to know about anything have a lot to learn. Being a writer is a continuous education. We learn each time we read; we learn each time we write.

I've heard fledgling writers say that they don't want to study because it might jeopardize the skills they already have. That's an arrogant stance. It's hard to imagine any education being harmful. Some of it may not be applicable, but none of it can be injurious.

All of us have much to learn about our craft. We can learn it from the masters, from the editors and publishers, and from our fellow writers. We can even learn it from our students.

Refusing to admit that can surely hamper progress.

"EDITORS HATE WRITERS IN GENERAL AND ME IN PARTICULAR"

Many of us believe that freelance writing is adversarial in nature. It's us against them. The writers against the editors. The talents against the know-nothings. Worse, we feel that they're the aggressors. The people in authority are dedicated to stamping out writers just as effectively as penicillin eliminates bacteria.

As we see it, agents get an office and a telephone so they can refuse to represent aspiring writers. Editors spend all their working hours concocting form rejection letters to send to writers. Publishers enjoy telling writers that their proposals don't fit into the company's editorial plans at this time, but they wish you luck in placing it elsewhere. And forget television producers. They neither read what you send, nor do they reply. They offer the ultimate snub: They ignore writers totally.

None of that is true, but some writers do believe it, and believing it can be problematic. You won't work on a crossword puzzle that has false clues; you won't struggle to solve a riddle if you know it has no answer; and you won't submit your best work to people who you honestly feel won't respect your writing.

These are only a few of the harmful attitudes that can infect the writer's mind and slow her progress.

How do you develop and maintain the right attitude? Be cold-bloodedly realistic — hopeful, but realistic. Select goals that are attainable. This doesn't mean you should sell yourself short or lower your goals just so they're easily attainable. Not at all. Remember Napoleon Hill's words: "Whatever the mind of man can conceive and believe, it can achieve." Shoot for the stars, but make sure — at least at first — they're stars that you can hit.

How can you detect harmful attitudes within yourself that might delay your progress? Again, be cold-bloodedly realistic and honest with yourself. List your biggest gripes about the writing profession in general and your career in particular. Be fiercely honest. Indulge yourself. Allow yourself to air all your complaints. Don't hold anything back; there's no reason to be genteel with this exercise.

Jot down all your peeves and rearrange them in logical order, the one that gripes you the most being first on your list.

Now analyze them. Are they justified or are they fabricated?

For instance, "Five editors have rejected my novel because the story line is weak" is justified. However, "Five editors have rejected my novel because they don't like California writers" is fabricated.

If your complaints are justified, work to correct the problem. In the first example above, you can study plotting techniques, take a writing course, read a book, or have another writer help you with the plot. You can correct the situation.

If your complaints are fabricated, you have an attitude problem. Take calm, logical, nonvindictive steps to correct that.

Investigate your complaints and analyze them, and you'll discover that you're working with fact instead of fantasy. If you're honest with yourself, you should induce an attitude change. This alteration can transform frustration into hope, despair into desire. You now have a goal to shoot for—one that you realize is far-reaching, but attainable. Your work should take on a new gusto, a new fire. You've shifted into high gear.

CHAPTER 3

GET INSPIRED

Most of the people I play tennis with at the local club are pleasantly mediocre. We all hit an occasional fantastic shot, flub more than a few, and otherwise hit average, harmless shots over the net, which are returned with average, harmless strokes. None of us plays incredibly intelligently, either. We go for winners when we should play safe and play safe when we should risk a winner. We hit short when we should hit deep, and cross court when traditional strategy advises down the line. We have fun playing a nice, middle-of-the road (although often fiercely competitive) game of tennis — except for one week of the year, Wimbledon week.

During the Wimbledon tournament, many of my opponents are transfigured into racquet-wielding terrors. They hit harder, better and smarter. They move with quickness, grace and balance. They seem to have added stamina, too. Why? Because they're inspired. They watch the matches on television and absorb not only the pomp and circumstance of that tournament, but also some of the skills and intelligence of the best professionals in the world. They don't take any extra lessons or practice any more, yet they play better. Why?

First, because they see the correct strokes and movement. They watch the game played correctly, and it registers in their own minds and in their own muscle memories. They now picture themselves moving and swinging like the pros do. Consequently, they *do* move better and stroke the ball properly more often.

Second, they see and appreciate intelligent strategy. Most professionals, even when they play badly, play by the book. They hit the right shots at the right time and to the right spot on the court. Amateurs don't. We convince ourselves that the dumb play is really the smart play. It isn't, but it doesn't hurt us as much because our opponents can't capitalize on our stupidity. The professionals can, and do. So when we observe, we begin to understand the logic behind certain strategies. The pros have learned from experience and from their coaches which is the safest play to make, the high-percentage play. When we amateurs see them play intelligently time after time, something clicks in our heads. We suddenly realize that maybe, after all, they are more knowledgeable than we are. Finally, we learn — at least for a little while.

Third, the pros fill us with hope. We see them hitting sizzling shots, chasing down balls that look "ungettable," performing feats that we considered impossible. Now, suddenly, we realize that those things *are* possible. Why should we just patty-cake the ball back, when we could drill it? Why should we stand back from the net and jab weakly at the ball, when we could move in and crunch a volley? Why should we concede a point to our opponent, when we can scramble a bit and perhaps keep the ball alive a little longer, maybe even win the point? We begin to see that with a minimum of additional effort, we can maximize our abilities.

Fourth, we gain an appreciation for the simplicity of genius and skill. We see excellence in players of normal size and shape. Oh sure, they're younger than we and better conditioned, but none is overpowering in comparison to each other. John McEnroe is not a Goliath to Ivan Lendl's David. No one in tennis can outmuscle an opponent. One player may have a slight edge in quickness or strength, but not an overwhelming edge.

What makes these professionals extraordinary is their consistency. They meet the ordinary demands of tennis extraordinarily well. They're always alert. They're always on balance. They anticipate their opponent's next play. It's all quite basic, quite simple. We begin to understand that we pedestrian players can raise our game a notch or two just by concentrating on the fundamentals.

Fifth, we get the courage to try everything we've learned. It looks uncomplicated; it looks easy. Why not try it? What have we got to lose?

Sixth, we get a fire in the pit of our stomachs. These players have shown us how it's done, and how beautiful it is when it's done correctly. We want to do that. We want to play a beautiful game of tennis, too.

All of this—the enlightenment, the education, the appreciation—adds up to inspiration. It's a yearning within us to duplicate, to the best of our ability, the genius of the masters. It's a tremendous incentive to improve our skills, and it works.

It works for a while, anyway. Most of my tennis pals eventually slide back to their comfortable level of mediocrity. They try to hit like the pros for a few games, but then decide it's easier to patty-cake the ball back. It's less effort, less trouble. That's why we're watching Wimbledon and not playing in it. But consider if my friends and I watched Wimbledon every week on television. Would our games improve dramatically? You bet they would.

Writers would improve, too, if they were constantly inspired by the captains of writing, the masters of their profession.

Everything we said about tennis applies to writing. You can be inspired, educated and goaded into improvement by "watching" the writing professionals at their craft. And good writing is easier to come by. Writers don't have to wait for the Wimbledon Tournament to be televised. Writers can pick up inspiration at the bookstore, at the library, at the movie theater, on television—almost anywhere, anytime.

If you're not happy with your writing success, find a writer who is where you would like to be and get inspired by her. Let her skills and her success light a fire under you and add energy to your career.

How do you get inspired?

Read Good Writing

Read those writers whom you admire or would most like to emulate. It's a simple and enjoyable process. These people write compellingly, so reading their works is fun. And when you read work you admire, you go through the same metamorphosis as my tennis buddies who watch the Wimbledon matches. You begin to absorb some of the writers' talent: how they develop plots and characters, how they use words, how they pique the reader — in general, how they use the tools of the profession. You begin to understand why they use certain devices, and when. You not only study how effective these tricks are, but you *feel* how effective they are. You begin to understand that you can write as well as they do, or at least that you can try to write with that same passion and technique. You appreciate the simplicity of great talent. You can see that well-written material reads easily. You get both the inspiration and the courage to try it.

Most writing teachers say there are only two ways to learn to write: to write, to write, and to write; and to read, to read, and to read. Read a lot of good writing, and you can't help but start to write better.

Read About Good Writers

Read about your favorites. My teachers used to say that reading was a magic carpet ride to any place in the world. It could transport you to the Middle East, Paris, Australia — anywhere. It can do that, but it can also introduce you to people you can never meet otherwise. You can walk with Thoreau along the banks of Walden Pond. You can sail with Melville on his whaling voyages. You can look over Jane Austen's shoulder as she writes her classic novels. You can get a feel for the genius of those writers you admire and discover how they achieved their success.

The closer you get to the giants of your profession, the more you're inspired by their genius. The more inspired you are, the harder and more efficiently you'll work to achieve your own success.

Visit Places Where Your Heroes Lived and Worked

Comedian Whoopi Goldberg does a funny but touching routine about visiting the home where Anne Frank lived before she was captured and incarcerated. Even listening to Whoopi's reenactment of her visit fills you with a sadness, yet a wonder, at the magnificent spirit of this little girl. Imagine how much more intense the feeling must be to actually stand in the room and live those emotions.

Any time you're in the presence of greatness—even if it's a presence once or twice removed—a little bit of it rubs off on you. Not the skills, necessarily, but the energy. It can inspire you to attack your own work with more gusto. That renewed vigor can improve your skills.

Visit Places You're Interested In

Go see places you might want to write about. If you enjoy writing about baseball, visit the Hall of Fame in Cooperstown, New York. Drink in all the memories and the memorabilia. Who knows? Maybe *Field of Dreams* was born of such reverie. If you write Westerns, visit some famous cowboy places—Dodge City, Tombstone, Kansas City. If you're a Civil War fanatic, visit the Gettysburg battlefield. Stories of bravery and heroism, of the soldiers and the families they left behind, might pop into your head as you roam over the fields.

No matter what you write, there is someplace that interests you. Experience it, live it, get inspired by it.

CHAPTER 4

KEEP MOVING FORWARD

Each year, as part of a medical examination, I submit to a mild, but humiliating, form of investigative torture. It even has an intimidating name — the stress test. It measures cardiovascular response to exertion.

It's humiliating because I first have to strip to the waist. For Arnold Schwarzenegger, this is acceptable; for me, it's mortifying. Then the technicians shave my chest — not all of it, just strategic areas. Further degradation, because for the next several weeks — around the swimming pool, at the beach, or just looking at myself in the mirror — I look like a dog with mange.

The shaving creates clear patches that receive the self-sticking sensors the technicians glue to my skin like so many mailing labels. Then they attach wires to each of these sensors, hooking me up to the electronic monitor. The outside of my body begins to look like the inside of my television set.

The sensors rarely stick, so they wrap the entire configuration with an ace bandage around my chest. They take a few measurements — heart rate, EKG, blood pressure — then stand me near the treadmill machine and ask if I'm ready to go. I've endured this much, so I nod okay.

Now the machine hums and gurgles, and the rubberized strip on the floor begins to move. I jump on and begin walking at the pace dictated by the machine. The machine is treacherous and relentless. It moves at a steady pace for three minutes, then it beeps. That beep warns that the pace not only will speed up, but the uphill angle will increase. I have to walk or jog faster, work a little harder. After three minutes the dastardly thing beeps again. More huffing, more puffing, more cursing under my breath, more sweat, more exertion.

The treadmill never tires. It's powered by electricity and can go forever, as fast and as steep as it likes. I have to keep up with it. It never asks, "Would you like me to go a little slower? Would you like to stop to catch your breath? Would you like to sit awhile and recover?" None of that. Its motor just keeps whirring. It has no soul.

If I stop to rest, what happens? The track keeps moving and I slide backward, off the treadmill, landing on my backside in a jumble of electrodes, wires and protestations from the health-care workers who are afraid I might have injured their delicate and expensive equipment.

Obviously, the test has to stop sometime. I tell them when I've reached my limit and they slow the treadmill to a comfortable stop. I get off and rest, and they record whatever readings they must. Actually, it's not a bad test, and neither the machine nor the test administrators are demonic pain merchants. I'm overdramatizing to make a point: that the road to writing success is not unlike that treadmill. It's rarely static. It's constantly in motion and seems to demand more and more activity to keep pace. Those who stop and rest find themselves not standing still, but drifting backward—losing ground instead of maintaining.

Success is not a place; it's a never-ending journey. It seems as though the further you advance, the harder you must work. Even if you get where you were going, you find out it's not really where you wanted to go. From there, you can see other horizons, more inviting pastures. You discover this was not really a goal at all, but a plateau on the way to your next achievement.

The journey allows little time for rest or for celebration at each plateau. It speeds up, elevates the incline, and urges you to move faster and work harder.

Picture your writing career as an ever-accelerating treadmill. You must keep moving forward.

There's no rest even for those who are sincerely and honestly happy where they are. Remember, the treadmill is moving backward, so you must jog forward just to remain stationery. You must exert yourself and struggle just to stay where you are. The cliché admonition in show business is: You're only as good as your last performance.

Earlier we said that the journey to your writing success was a series of plateaus. You struggle along at the same level for some time, feeling as though you're making little or no progress, then suddenly you jump to the next plateau. It's an exhilarating victory. However, it's one that allows little time for relaxation and recuperation.

The treadmill beeps. You find yourself running at a faster pace up a steeper incline. Rather than meriting a rest, you've earned the right to work harder.

We've all heard the aphorism, "A little knowledge is a dangerous thing." A person with a little knowledge thinks he knows it all. He might not only stop learning more, but he can occasionally make an ass of himself. C'mon—we've all been guilty of it.

A touch of success can be treacherous, too, for the same reason. When we get a little success, we think we have it all. We coast. We get content. We get smug. I once overheard two producers talking about a well-known writer and one said, "He's no good anymore." The other asked, "Why?" The first answered, "Because he's become a writer."

The implication was that this person no longer wrote from the gut. The writing lost the emotions and the feel of the common person; it was done from the point of view of a successful, well-paid writer.

Complacency, if we allow it a foothold, destroys the desire we once had. We're no longer ambitious, driven, hungry.

When I first arrived in Hollywood, I confessed to my mentor, Phyllis Diller, that I was somewhat awed and frightened by the city. She told me: "You'll be all right, so long as you don't become a fat-assed Hollywood writer."

She was warning me that the journey wasn't over. All this step did was put me into the fray. It opened up opportunities for me, but it guaranteed none. If I wanted to stay in the business, I had to continue to prove myself. I had to keep working at it.

Sometimes our writing careers stall because we try to coast. We try to sit back and enjoy the fruits of our labor instead of continuing our labor. It's difficult because the treadmill keeps moving.

But if this sounds more like torture than fun, then my treadmill analogy has failed. You can progress at a more leisurely pace in your writing career than you would on a treadmill. You can enjoy the journey as you go. Each plateau should be its own reward.

The treadmill comparison is merely to remind you that to progress, to keep moving forward, you must keep the desire alive. You must keep burning whatever pilot light it was that got you started as a writer in the first place. Whatever success you've enjoyed until now, there is more waiting for you. But you must work to get it. You must keep putting one foot in front of the other on the treadmill.

When the treadmill starts getting ahead of you, here are a few suggestions that you might try to keep your career moving forward. A few of these ideas will be expanded in their own chapters later in the book, but I'll list them briefly here.

DEVELOP YOUR WRITING SKILLS

Writing is a many-faceted craft. It requires imagination, precision, clarity, a sense of reality, a sense of fun. At times it demands a scientist's accuracy, at other times a con man's charm. More often than not it necessitates a combination of the two.

Many techniques and skills are related to writing. No one can possibly master them all. Even if one manages to qualify as expert in all of them, she can't be expert to the same degree in all of them. By definition, every writer must have certain strengths and weaknesses.

It seems logical that developing, strengthening, and improving those areas where your skills are weakest would also improve your writing. The whole is still equal to the sum of its parts. Your writing is the product of all your skills combined.

Once I was warming up with a tennis opponent before a match. In warming up for tennis, players hit some shots back and forth to loosen up the muscles, perfect the timing, and just get used to the feel of the ball on the racquet. Normally the players hit a few shots from the baseline; then one steps to the net to practice a few volleys, then hits a few overhead smashes. This particular day, I asked my opponent if he'd like a few overheads. He said, "No thanks. I'm lousy at hitting overheads, so I never practice them."

That logic confounded me. It seemed to me he should have spent more time practicing the shot that he had the most trouble with. That's the only way you develop a well-rounded, all-inclusive tennis game. And perfecting the overhead would enhance all the other shots in this player's arsenal, because it would improve his overall game.

In the same way, developing every skill related to your writing—especially those in which you feel the weakest—enhances your overall writing technique. Therefore, it's a good idea to devote some time each day—not your entire writing-time budget, but a half hour or an hour—to developing some particular skill related to your writing.

For example, you might study vocabulary. Learn more words and a greater variety of synonyms. Not so you can use bigger, more complicated words, but so you'll more readily have access to the correct word, the perfect word. I think it was Mark Twain who said that the difference between the right word and the almost-right word was the difference between "lightning" and "lightning bug."

Do you have trouble creating colorful, vibrant descriptions? Devote some time to improving that skill. Formulate exercises that will help you to write better descriptions. The more you train, the better you get, and the better your writing will be.

How about bright, witty similes? Are they difficult for you? Practice them. Is the ability to plot good stories your trouble spot? Work on it. Do you have trouble developing believable characters? Study how the experts do it, practice, and perfect your own technique.

There are any number of areas where you could use improvement. You know them better than anyone else. Devote time to them. Work on them. Improve them. As you improve any part of your writing, you improve the whole of your writing. You stay one step ahead of that treadmill.

BEHAVE AS IF YOU'RE ALREADY ON THE NEXT PLATEAU

Please don't jump to the conclusion that this is some kind of self-help, autohypnotic type of mumbo jumbo where you reach down and pick yourself up by your own bootstraps. It's not. Nevertheless, there are some benefits to behaving as if you've already arrived where you want to be. If you want to be a syndicated columnist, behave like a syndicated columnist. If you want to be a novelist, behave like a successful novelist. Whatever you want to be—think, feel and act like that person.

When you think, feel and act like the person you want to be, you begin to convince yourself that you *can* be that person. You begin to develop the mind-set of that person. You begin to see things and do things the way that person sees and does things. What is important to that person becomes important to you. Consequently, you begin to write more like that person, too.

Understand, there's no fraud or deception implied in this suggestion. You're not to represent yourself as a successful novelist when you haven't had a book published. You're not to manufacture an impressive list of bogus credits to impress potential buyers. No, I'm speaking of internalization. It's getting a "feel" for your next writing plateau. In your mind, your heart and your soul, you become what you want to be. This makes you think and feel that way, which makes you act that way, which helps you write that way.

So it pays to begin developing the mind-set now. Start thinking, feeling and acting like the person you want to be, and you may just outsmart the treadmill.

GO BACK TO BASICS

It's ironic, but one of the surest ways to move forward is to move backward—to return to the basics. Anything, regardless of how complex, can be broken down to its components, reduced to the fundamentals.

Golf is an extremely complicated sport. Anyone who plays the game on weekends knows that there are many more bad ways to hit the ball than there are good ways to hit it. Yet, when you watch the pros play on television and listen to the experts analyze their swings, you realize that the golf swing is nothing more than a series of basic motions. The experts talk about the grip, the stance, the positioning of the ball, the takeaway, the downswing, the contact point, the follow-through. They're all basic components of the golf stroke. If each is perfect, the swing and the hit are perfect. If one is faulty, the entire stroke collapses.

The experts look to the fundamentals, too, to correct flaws. If one pulls the ball to the right, he checks the grip. Perhaps his right hand is turned too much on the shaft. The golf doctors have a list of possible ailments for each symptom, and they all relate back to the fundamentals.

The same is true for writers, except that we sometimes forget that our skills also are based in fundamentals. The further we progress in our profession, the more compelling is the temptation to abandon the basics. Basics, we feel, are for beginners, neophytes, amateurs. But that's not the case.

Like the golf swing, writing is a collection of basics. If the fundamentals are perfected, the writing becomes more mature. Fundamentals might include outlining a piece before writing it to ensure clarity of presentation; knowing and following solid rules of sentence structure, punctuation, grammar and style; researching vocabulary to be certain that you use the right word and not the almost-right word.

A writer should learn to analyze her product the same way a golfer analyzes his swing. Recognize and admit to the flaws, research backward to the fundamental that's causing the fault, and then work on that basic. Practice it until you eliminate the defect.

Of course, the golfer has one luxury that the writer doesn't: The bad shot usually is obvious. If a golfer hooks a ball deep into the woods, that's a bad swing. The writer's flaws are not so glaring. That's why you must begin by reading your own writing with a critical eye and being fiercely honest about it.

If your lead doesn't entice the reader into your copy, you need more work on your opening. If the copy feels monotonous, your sentences may be too similar in structure or length; they might need more variety. If the copy doesn't sparkle, you may want to find stronger, more descriptive verbs.

First, be honest about your writing, and then be thorough in investigating the source or possible sources of the problem. Read up on it. Try different approaches until you find one that works for you. Work to correct the fault. Practice what you lack.

Going backward—to the fundamentals—is one way to ensure going forward and keeping pace with the relentless treadmill.

ENGAGE IN ANOTHER FORM OF WRITING

Familiarity breeds contempt. It also can breed boredom and apathy. Do a thing often enough, and you grow to hate it. You get fed up with doing it and lose interest in doing it well. At least, that's the tendency.

Of course, this doesn't always extend to the extremes. If you tighten nuts and bolts on an assembly line for eight hours a day, it doesn't mean that at the end of the day you go totally berserk, put the wrong sized bolts into the wrong sized nuts, and disrupt the entire assembly line. But your efficiency can suffer slightly.

The same can apply to writing. Most of us tend to write the same sort of piece over and over again. We specialize. Some write journalistic articles, others write children's books. Some write humor, some biography. Professionally, there's nothing wrong with this. Specialization is a natural result of our marketing. If we tend to write good medical articles, we sell more medical articles. We get a good reputation with health-care publishers. That's simply the business of writing.

However, it does take on the "assembly line" attributes. It can breed contempt, boredom and possibly an indifference about your work. Again, not to the extreme, but perhaps just enough to affect the quality of your work.

One way to counteract this is to work on different types of writing. This work doesn't have to be for the marketplace. It can simply be for your own refreshment, to keep you from getting stale in your professional writing.

If you write and sell heavily researched articles for magazines, try writing some pieces for children. Try writing some Jay Leno-type one-liners. One writer I know begins each writing day with a limerick. He sells none of them, but never turns to his professional writing tasks until he has composed five lines of verse that satisfy him. He finds it therapeutic. It's refreshing, and he feels that it clears his mind and guarantees that he's now ready for serious writing.

It's not a bad idea. It's almost like fifteen or twenty minutes of relaxation before beginning the workday.

You can select any genre you like, or even vary it each day. One day write a sonnet, another day a limerick, perhaps a short story, or a short piece of humor. Whatever you select, it should be different from your workaday writing. It's a device that can not only refresh your mind, but also sharpen your skills in other areas. Sometimes you'll find that those sharper skills are reflected in your professional writing.

Athletes call this technique cross-training. It seems to help them; it can help you, too — to keep your writing career moving on that unyielding treadmill.

STRETCH YOUR PRESENT WRITING

Success is like the horizon. It's always out there in the distance. It's in plain view, but it's unreachable. No matter how diligently you approach it, it always remains a safe distance away.

No matter how far you've progressed in your writing career, you're never where you want to be or where you feel you should be. Each conquest opens up more inviting challenges. Your goal is always in the distance, like the horizon.

Rather than being demoralizing, this is exciting. In writing there's always another challenge to be met, another goal to be reached. You'll never run out of new plateaus to traverse, new frontiers to explore.

Now is the time to move forward. Wherever you stand on this earth, you can see a horizon. Whatever kind of writing success you enjoy, there is a further goal contained within it. You have to define that goal—it's a personal thing—and begin to reach for it. If you write magazine short stories, the next goal may be a published novel. If you write genre fiction, a mainstream book may be your next adventure. You must define the next plateau and begin moving in that direction.

You can maintain your present writing success and still allocate a certain percentage of your time to the pursuit of the next plateau. A successful band leader once advised: "Work part of your day for today and part of your day for tomorrow."

That's what writers can do to keep the treadmill moving. Devote a certain percentage of your workday—whatever you can budget for that purpose—to chasing the horizon, to pursuing your next goal.

SELECT ANOTHER GOAL

Sometimes, the horizon is not the direction you want to go. You may stand and gaze at the horizon and yearn to travel to China, Africa, Indonesia—somewhere where the horizon is totally hidden from your view.

The same may be true of your writing. You may see plateaus ahead of you that hold no fascination. Fine. There's nothing wrong with changing directions. If you're a promising novelist but you want to be a poet, start devoting time to your poetry. Let your fiction pay your bills while your poetry fuels your dreams.

The American dream preserves this fallacy that once we begin a journey we must continue to its natural conclusion. If you begin your career in sales, you must progress from salesperson to regional sales manager to district sales manager to national sales manager to vice-president in charge of sales, perhaps to CEO.

There's no guarantee, though, that every regional sales manager wants to be national sales manager. Oh, I know that logic says he should. Family and friends say the same thing. However, this particular regional sales manager may want to become a ski instructor, or a rock musician, or the proprietor of a local shop that sells funny T-shirts and hats to tourists.

Changing goals and dreams is a free person's prerogative. That includes writers.

You don't have to stay on that same treadmill. You can hop off and jump onto another one, pointed in a different direction. That choice is yours.

MAINTAIN THE QUANTITY AND QUALITY OF YOUR WRITING

There's one infallible gimmick that guarantees success in writing (and practically any other field): Be good, and keep getting better.

If a writer does nothing more than constantly improve her quantity and quality of work, she'll remain well ahead of the pack, and well ahead of the treadmill.

CHAPTER 5

MAKE THINGS HAPPEN

The second contract I landed in television was on the staff of "Laugh-In." I did nothing to get the job. I was just lucky. Phyllis Diller appeared on the show and she brought some of my one-liners for her monologue. The producer liked the material, saw my letterhead on Phyllis's script, jotted down my number, and called to offer me the job. I took it.

It prompted me to ask the other writers on the show how they got their jobs, because some of them were first-time television writers. One young writer told me he had tried to set up a meeting with the producer to show some of his material. The producer was hard to contact. When this writer finally did speak with the producer about an interview, the producer was agreeable, but very busy. The scheduled meeting was always canceled or postponed. Finally, the writer sent the producer an entire script for "Laugh-In," complete with guest stars, gags for the "joke wall," cocktail party—every element of the show. The script was about 150 pages long. The producer was impressed with the industry and the inventiveness of this young writer. He read the script, or at least enough of it to be impressed with the quality of the writing, too. The following season, this writer was a member of the "Laugh-In" writing staff.

"Laugh-In" was a top-rated show at that time and was respected by writers. Veterans as well as newcomers wanted to be hired for it. Why did this novice land the assignment when others didn't? One reason was that he didn't just sit around and wait for something to happen. He wasn't idle while waiting for the meeting with the producer to materialize. He was doing something. He was building material to show that he could write comedy for this program. Eventually, he assembled enough material to fill an entire script and he sent it to the producer.

It worked. He made things happen.

Writers' lives are filled with agonizing waits, and we sometimes suspend animation waiting for word on our last project. We're lulled into nonproductivity by the slowness of the editor's responses: "Oh yes, I know I told you I would have an answer for you last Thursday but that was before we scheduled a meeting this Thursday to decide to talk about your project at next Thursday's meeting. I'll call you with an answer a couple of Thursdays from next Thursday." We begin to feel like some poor commuter who has the correct change ready, but the bus is not coming.

Today has twenty-four hours in it, whether you get the letter or the phone call you were expecting or not. Today has 1,440 usable minutes in it, whether that short story you sent out sold or didn't sell. With some creativity and logical planning, a writer can find something to do on a past project, a present project or a future project — right now, today.

Here are a few suggestions to make things happen.

FOLLOW UP ON A PROJECT

Editors are proud of their discipline. I've attended writing seminars and shared the platform with many editors at writing workshops. Countless times I've heard, "I respond to all queries within four weeks and all manuscripts within two months." They proclaim this with the same fervor as Patton addressing his troops.

I've written to some of these editors and never heard from them again. A few I've written to two or three times and never heard from again. I have one series of letters spread across my desk right now in which I initiated contact with a query letter in December 1990. No response. I inquired again in March 1991. I received a response in June 1991 in which the editor apologized for the delay but explained that things were hectic at the editorial offices. He would get back to me with a response soon. That's the last letter in the folder.

This is not to condemn editors. They mean well, but they have inordinate demands on their time. Take a look at your desk top right now. As disorganized and overcrowded as it is, the editor's is as bad or worse. So it is with understanding and for-giveness that we realize they can't always meet their commitments. Nevertheless, they're holding your manuscript—a manuscript that's worthwhile and could be making the rounds to other editors instead of playing hide-and-seek on their desk top.

Make things happen. Give them a call and inquire or write a follow-up letter.

Some editors may bark and grumble at this. "My time is at a premium already. I can't afford to waste any more of it chatting to you on the phone or explaining myself in a senseless letter." Perhaps you can send a self-addressed, stamped postcard with possible responses on the back so the editor can check those that apply. It shows that you realize their time is at a premium.

But the writer's time is at a premium, too. The difference is that editors are paid at the end of each week regardless of whether they respond to our inquiries. Freelancers only get paid when the manuscript sells.

If you don't get a response, it's your obligation to find out why. I once wrote a query letter to a publishing house suggesting a book. I said if they were interested I could send a formal proposal almost immediately. I never heard from them and wrote them off.

Two years later, the acquisitions editor called me. She explained that she had asked an editor to respond to me and request the proposal. When this editor left the company, they found the folder in his desk. He had never contacted me. They thought it was me who was snubbing them.

We did the book, and since then I've contracted for six other books with the same company. However, the mix-up could have been avoided if I had only called or written a follow-up letter.

Most editors are reasonable. In fact, most editors sincerely care about writers and their work. They enjoy working with writers and buying material from them. They want to see talented new writers succeed. Most will gladly respond to your inquiries and follow-ups as quickly as possible.

The writer must be reasonable, too. If an editor promises to respond in four weeks, you can't pounce on him with angry invectives on the twenty-ninth day. Allow a reasonable grace period. Take a look at your desk top again to understand why. However, if you don't receive some sort of response after a reasonable time, bother him. Be polite, but be persistent. Remember, it's your career, not his.

MOVE ON TO YOUR NEXT PROJECT

Some writers complain that the curse of their profession is the blank sheet of paper. It's so stark, so naked. It stares up at them in defiance. It says, "I'm pure. I'm clean. Whatever ink you put on me had better be justified. It had better be worthwhile." It's intimidating.

That same blank sheet, though, can be the blessing of our business. It's white, virginal. It comes to us with no prejudices, no preassigned ideas. The blank sheet offers no criticism, no condemnation. It's neutral. It says to the writer, "Here I am. Write on me whatever you feel inspired to write."

Regardless of what else is going on in a writer's professional or personal life, there is always a blank sheet of paper waiting to receive the next article, story, script or poem. Let's say the response to your last query letter wasn't exactly a turndown, but it was lukewarm. So what? You can still begin work on a new project. Maybe your book has finally been published and sales seem encouraging. Congratulations. Get working on the sequel. Perhaps you've got three or four manuscripts in limbo—some editor has each of them, but you're getting nothing in the mail. All right. Get working on your next opus, so you can mail it into limbo, too.

Writing is a personal profession. All the freelancer needs is a place to work and a keyboard to tap. No matter what sort of winds are raging at the time, the writer can always retreat to the office, insert a blank sheet of paper, and begin typing, "It was the best of times; it was the worst of times."

FIND NEW IDEAS IN YOUR PAST WORK

"Big oaks from little acorns grow." It is amazing that the potential for a giant tree is contained within the shell of a tiny little nut. The reverse, though, is just as astounding: how many acorns a giant oak contains.

Writers can harvest the acorns from some of their oak trees.

A speaker at a magazine-writing seminar I attended once said that every good article should yield, with some effort and creativity on the author's part, at least three more good article ideas. For example, if you write a piece about General Custer and the famous Battle of Little Bighorn, you might now write one on the Sioux and Cheyenne chiefs at the same battle. How did they prepare for the encounter? What military expertise did they display?

Following the same strategy, you might also do an article on the battlefield as it appears today. What articles sell best in the gift shops there? Who are the tourists who come there?

You might also do a hypothetical piece. What would have happened if this battle had never taken place? Would George Custer have gone on to become President? Would the Cheyenne and Sioux have gone to the reservations or rebelled and fought again later?

Perhaps there's a historical novel lying in embryo within this article. How would Custer's and Chief Sitting Bull's lives have progressed? You might even invent a dramatic confrontation for them later in their lives.

In any case, you see how one idea can contain the germ of another. Combing through past successes for ideas that could generate future successes is another way of making things happen.

STUDY TO IMPROVE YOUR CRAFT

When my grandson was about four years old, his mom enrolled him in a youngsters' tennis clinic. It was a basic series of lessons, little more than how to hold the racquet and behave on the court. He enjoyed them, though.

Later, I went to the court to hit a few balls with him and asked if he might sign up for lessons again the following season. He said, "No, I know all there is to know about tennis now."

Many of us, much older than age four and slightly more mature, adopt the same attitude. "I know all there is to know about writing." We don't.

One way to make things happen in our careers is to get smarter, to learn more about our craft. And no matter how much we learn, we'll always have more to learn.

We'll talk of learning more about your craft in a later chapter, but for now be aware that any education you can get about the writing business will help make things happen.

MAKE CONTACTS

In so many professions the cliché "It's not what you know but who you know" is at least partially true. Influential friends in high places do help. So a writer can make things happen by cultivating a few.

A writer I once knew was a real scamp. He dated almost every young woman in town and no matter where you went with him, women would come over to chat. Whenever you saw him he was carrying on a conversation with a smiling young lady. He was an available bachelor and was making the most of it.

I asked him once how he managed to meet so many women. He said, "Whenever I see a woman that I'm attracted to, I say hello to her. After that I just ad-lib."

"Hello" was his universal introduction. It was the start of a conversation and often the beginning of a friendship. As writers, we sometimes have to begin making friends with a "hello."

The important lesson to be learned from my roguish friend

is that he initiated the contact. He didn't wish that someone would come and talk to him; he talked to her. He offered a friendly greeting and then let it progress from there in whatever direction it chose.

We sometimes need to contact people. We need to offer the first greeting. Here are some ways to make things happen by meeting people in the writing profession.

Write Letters

Twenty-nine cents — or whatever the postal rates have risen to by the time you read this — is a relatively cheap way to cultivate new friends. I have many acquaintances in writing whom I first met through the mail. Either I wrote to them or they wrote to me, we exchanged a few ideas by letter, and we eventually met and continued the friendship.

A colleague of mine liked an article she read in a magazine. She wrote to the author congratulating her on a job well done. The author called to thank my friend, learned that she also was a writer, and asked to see some of her work. As a result, the author recommended this writer to several of her editors. One letter led to several magazine assignments and at least one book sale to date.

That's making things happen.

Attend Seminars, Conferences and Workshops

A few years back I went to Dodger Stadium with my daughter to pick our seats for the upcoming season. Our host offered us two choices. The first was in the upper deck right along first base. It offered a good view of the action on the field. The second choice was right on the field level, about five rows back, but out in right field. They offered a close-up, but distorted, view of the game.

I wanted the upper-deck seats; my daughter wanted to be on the field. I said, "But you can see the game better from the upper deck." She said, "Dad, you can't meet and marry a rich baseball player from the upper deck."

If you want to meet people in writing, you must go where the writers are. Attend writing seminars, conferences and workshops; the people you admire and want to meet will be there, either as faculty or participants. Introduce yourself—remember, begin with hello and then ad-lib—and talk to the writers, editors and agents who lecture at these events.

Volunteer

You can work as a volunteer at these same seminars, conferences and workshops. Be an envelope stuffer. Be a lecturer. Offer to serve on the faculty or judge some of the writing contests. Besides meeting other people who are as interested in writing as you are, you'll meet some of the profession's influential people: authors, editors and agents. These people might help you make things happen.

Don't misunderstand, though. Meeting influential people in the profession won't automatically advance your career. You must impress them with your dedication and your talent. The best way to do that is to be dedicated and talented.

MAP OUT A CAREER STRATEGY

First, honestly analyze and evaluate your writing and your career. Try to step back the way a painter does to get a perspective on her brushstrokes, and honestly and dispassionately assess your talent. Are you as good as you think you are? How does your work compare to other works in the same genre? Note your strengths and how you can better capitalize on them. Recognize your weaknesses. Also, reexamine the direction of your career. Are you happy doing the kind of writing you're doing, or would you rather pursue another genre?

Second, figure out ways to improve your writing. You might take some classes or join a local workshop. You might devise exercises of your own that will help strengthen the weaker aspects of your writing. If you want your career to head in a different direction, start doing some work that will lead you in this new direction.

Third, set long-range goals. Decide as honestly as you can where you want your career to be a year or so down the line, then plan how to get it there. Just as you would map out a cross-country automobile trip, you should map out some career goals and plan your strategy.

Again, it's making things happen.

CHAPTER 6

BE THE WRITER YOU WANT TO BECOME

This chapter has magic and secrecy in it. The magic is that it will be your Fairy Godmother (or Fairy Godfather, if there are male activists among the readers). Do you want to be the writer of legendary children's books? This chapter waves its magic wand and you are now the writer of legendary children's books. Do you want to be a newspaper columnist? These pages will sprinkle magic dust about your head. Presto! You're a newspaper columnist. Novelist? Poof! You're a novelist. Travel writer, you say? No problem. Zap! Pack your bags. Simply think which kind of writer you want to become, and these magical pages will make you that writer . . . immediately . . . effortlessly. That's the magic of this chapter.

The *secret* of this chapter is that you don't need the magic of this chapter. You can do all this on your own. Yes, immediately. Yes, effortlessly. All you do is think of the writer you want to become and then become that writer.

Do this by beginning to think, feel and act like the writer you want to be. If you want to be the author of romance novels, dress like a romance novelist would dress, think like a romance novelist would think, read what a romance novelist would read. Finally, of course, you'll write what a romance novelist would write.

Yes, it is play-acting, pretending. It is a bit of mental trickery. Probably, in the strictest interpretation, it's slightly deceitful. However, you're only deceiving yourself. You're trying to convince yourself that you're a little better than you thought you were.

Or, *are* you being deceitful? It just might be that you have the potential to be the writer you want to become, and you're deceiving yourself into thinking you don't. Your fears and insecurities might be holding you back. Thinking, feeling and acting like the writer you want to be may be more honest than you think.

Please, though, don't slam this book shut and dismiss it as more of that "self-help" pap. That's not what this chapter suggests. Admittedly, the power of positive thinking is central to most self-help philosophies. Norman Vincent Peale says, "Change your thoughts and you change your world." Frank Lloyd Wright suggests, "The belief in a thing makes it happen." Lily Tomlin adds humor to the same principle: "I always wanted to be somebody, but I should have been more specific."

These ideas may or may not be valid. You must decide whether to subscribe to them. They are, however, beyond the scope of this writing book. I'm limiting my advice to hard-nosed, practical ideas that will get your career moving as rapidly as possible in the right direction. If thinking, feeling and acting like the person you want to become have a metaphysical value, that's a fringe benefit. Certainly all of us will accept any bonuses. However, this phenomenon also has pragmatic worth.

I first discovered its value in a nonwriting environment. Before becoming a writer I worked for an electrical manufacturing company. I began as an electrical drafting apprentice and then graduated to electrical draftsman and electrical designer. Those were natural, almost automatic, progressions. You got those if you did a reasonably competent job and didn't cause trouble.

The next step was a formidable one: to "Supervisor." It was from union worker to nonunion, from nonexempt to exempt, from labor to management. It was a promotion reserved for a select few. It was a desirable promotion because it not only brought more prestige and more money, but it also got you a parking space within five blocks of the plant.

Several of my contemporaries got this promotion ahead of me. I was usually on the list of candidates, but never got the nod. Then I began to notice a pattern. The people who made the selection always chose someone who resembled themselves. The management team was required to wear ties, so they preferred someone from the labor force who wore a tie. They picked people who came to work early and stayed a little late to complete a task, even though good union employees always left when the quitting whistle blew. They promoted those workers who were concerned not just with getting the job done, but with getting it done well, with cost reduction and customer satisfaction in mind. In other words, they picked the workers who thought and acted like supervisors already.

Well, I didn't have to get hit with a ton of bricks (too often) to see reality. I began to think, feel and act as if I were a supervisor. I wasn't appointed to the next opening, but I got the one after that. I was finally made supervisor.

I then applied what I learned to my writing. Within nine months of getting my promotion, I left the company to write full time. The commonsense advantages I learned about corporate promotions also influenced my writing.

Here are some of the pragmatic results of thinking, feeling and acting like the writer you want to become.

IT SHARPENS YOUR AWARENESS

I'm always astounded with the perception of travel writers. I've been to many places, but I have no definitive opinions of them. "How was Tahiti?" people ask. "It was nice," I say. "It's more primitive than Hawaii, but the people were nice." "How was the food?" they ask. "The food was nice," I say. They ask about the flight over and back. Naturally, I say, "The flight over and back was nice — long, but nice." "Were there a lot of insects and critters over there?" "Yes," I say, "there were insects and critters, but they were nice."

Travel writers see much more than I see and they verbalize it. When I read what they write, I realize that I saw all of that, too; it just didn't register. It registers with them because they think like travel writers. They've trained their minds and their senses to notice these items. It becomes second nature to them — and to you, when you begin to think, feel and act as if you were a travel writer.

Let me go back to my drafting days to give you an example of how this happens. As a draftsman, I worked on an average of two assignments a week. These assignments were customized so each had variations. They were identified by a "shop order" number. When someone from the factory questioned me about a job, I would look up the shop order number, dig out the folder and refresh my memory. I couldn't remember numbers and equate them to the specifics of the assignment.

When I became supervisor, I was responsible for about thirty to forty-five shop order numbers each week. I never consciously did anything to change my thinking or my memory capacity, yet when someone would ask about job #911045, I'd immediately know the details of the job, the status of the job, and when it was scheduled to be completed and shipped to the customer. Without any effort on my part, I remembered more than I ever could as a draftsman.

Why? How? I don't know. The reason, though, was that I was a supervisor. I had the responsibility. I had to think, feel and act like a supervisor because that's what I was.

We've all been to parties and met many interesting people. We've also met flaky people, eccentric people, funny people, frightening people and angry people. To most of us they're just folks whom we meet and talk with in passing. Not to novelists, though. These are people whom novelists will dissect. They'll extract characteristics from one person and cross-pollinate him with the idiosyncrasies of another. From this cross-pollination they'll breed a new, intriguing character for their next book. In fact, a fragment of one conversation may suggest to them the beginning of a premise for their next novel.

You and I think and react like ordinary people; the novelist thinks and reacts like a novelist. He's more attuned to people, more perceptive. He's extraordinary. When you start to think like a novelist, you'll start seeing character traits and hearing dialogue that you never noticed before.

You and I have visited interesting places and we react the way I reacted to Tahiti: "It's nice." But I know a screenwriter who filters everything she sees and every place she visits as a potential locale for her next screenplay. To her, the famous aquarium in Monterey is not just a place where you see fish and learn about marine life. No—to her, it's a backdrop for a frenetic cops-and-robbers chase. A butcher shop is not just a place where meat is trimmed and cut; it's a locale where detectives question a suspect, who just happens to be a butcher. She once saw a teddy bear factory and thought it would be an ideal setting for a love scene. She has trained herself to look beyond the obvious and to see every place as a possible locale for some scene or another in her next film. If you become a screenwriter, you'll begin to view settings through those same creative eyes.

IT EXPEDITES YOUR EDUCATION

Many people, when they read an especially good novel, enjoy talking about it—about the characters, the plot, the locale. They'll even give away the ending and save you the trouble of reading it. Sometimes you can stump them, though, by asking, "Was it written in the first person or the third person?"

Often they won't know. That's good. They're so caught up in the story and so captivated by the writing that they weren't distracted by technical details. But writers who have begun to think, feel and act like a novelist want to know all the details of the writing. Which character told the story? Were flashbacks used? How? In which locales did the various scenes take place?

And writers who have begun to think, feel and act like a novelist will note these details, file them away, and use them later in writing their own fiction.

Readers will not notice how good magazine articles hook their readers with the first paragraph; nonfiction writers will.

Viewers won't notice how subtleties in a film reveal character traits; a screenwriter will.

Good writers learn from the works of other good writers. That's their education, their classroom. However, you must have your antennae up to notice these lessons and learn from them. By seeing yourself as the writer you want to become, you'll prepare yourself to observe more and learn more.

IT INFLUENCES YOUR WORK HABITS

Read an article about any writer, and you'll generally learn that writer has a disciplined schedule. One will wake early and write for three solid hours. Another will relax in the mornings, but write all afternoon. Some write when the rest of the world sleeps. The details don't matter. What matters is that they all have a work routine that they follow.

They have to. You don't turn out ten or twelve great novels by writing only when you feel like it. Screenplays don't flow out of the typewriter only when the spirit moves the writer. Magazine articles don't happen without research, planning and, yes, writing.

A good writer has an organized writing agenda. Amateurs' "organized plans" too often are something they have penciled in to do in the future.

A friend once gave me a completed novel to read. I enjoyed it but was in no position to edit or evaluate it. I simply told him it was enjoyable. He told me that he had sent it out to several publishers and they all recommended restructuring and extensive rewriting. He said, "I don't want to do any rewriting on this book until it sells."

It's the chicken-and-egg riddle all over again. He won't sell the book unless he rewrites, and he won't rewrite until he sells the book. Don't look for it in your bookstore in the near future.

I wish I had one dollar for everyone who has told me, "You should see what I have to go through every day. I could write a book." They all have the Great American Novel within them, or their autobiography, which they swear is not only unique but has unlimited sales appeal. These people will never write these books because they just will never write these books. They don't begin an outline. They don't roll the paper into the typewriter and start tapping the keys. They'll do it, they think, when they have some time.

Writers don't do that. Writers write. Playwrights write plays. Screenwriters write films. Novelists write novels. Other writers write magazine articles, poems, children's books, whatever.

When you begin to think, feel and act like the writer you want to become, you'll plan your schedule. You'll turn out pages of your novel instead of wishing that someday you could get started on it. You'll start writing that newspaper column you've always thought about syndicating. You'll assemble your poems into a collection for publication. You'll complete your short story.

Successful writers would have a schedule to complete these projects. Since you now think and act like a successful writer, you will, too.

IT INFLUENCES THE IMAGE YOU PROJECT

Becoming, in your mind, the writer you want to be will prompt you to change your image. Which type of letterhead would a successful writer in your genre have? You'll have the same. A successful writer would present her manuscripts on neatly typed, error-free pages. You will, too. A successful writer would think about the kind of printer appropriate for her type of writing. Rather than select the cheapest printer, a successful writer would have one that best represents her work. That's the kind of printer you'll want.

These are mechanical items—things you can buy or have done for you. However, your own presentations—those you generate from your creativity—will change for the better, also.

If you believe yourself to be a successful writer, your query letters will be more compact, more professional. They won't have that whining, pleading tone of some amateurs. They'll be confident, self-assured and businesslike. They'll get to the point, state the premise, and be done with it.

At my former company, it was the tie that told the powers that be, "I am supervisor material." With writers, every piece of correspondence you send out, every manuscript, should wear a tie.

IT AFFECTS THE INDUSTRY'S PERCEPTION OF YOU

In the writing industry, there are people whose job is to buy a product: good, solid, professional manuscripts. For the most part, they have neither the time, the money, nor the inclination to train potential writers. They want pros.

When you begin to think, feel and act like the writer you want to become, you give off the odor of professionalism. You smell like a writer. The buyers feel like they can trust you to deliver. That's priceless.

IT AFFECTS YOUR WRITING

Remember how I told you when I became a supervisor I could recall the many jobs I was responsible for? I don't know how I did it; I just did. Your writing improves when you believe yourself to be the writer you want to be. I don't know how or why it does; it just does.

Whatever force runs this universe has a hunger for balance. If you look like a duck, walk like a duck, and quack like a duck, nature makes you a duck. So why not begin now to look, walk and quack like whatever kind of writer you want to become?

CHAPTER 7

GET YOURSELF IN SHAPE

I work at home, which is a fantastic luxury. I can roll out of bed and into my workplace without fighting freeway cranks, without shaving, often without even bothering to change from my pajamas. In fact, when I walk into the living room dressed even in casual clothes in the morning, my family usually asks, "Where are you going?"

However, the office at home confuses my grandchildren. My daughter took one of her youngsters—a kindergartner—to a meeting at school. During the discussion the word "retirement" was used. My grandson asked his mom, "What is retirement?" She explained, "It's when people get older and they stop working." My grandson said, "Oh, you mean like Grandpop?"

My daughter defended me and my work habits. She explained, "Grandpop isn't retired. He still works. He just works at home." My grandson thought about this awhile and then said, "He doesn't work. He only types."

Some writers make the same mistake. We assume that typing isn't work. It is. Thinking burns calories. Creating demands energy. Writing can be a strenuous activity. Whether it demands as much stamina as digging ditches or as much endurance as an athletic event is immaterial. It is toil and it requires conditioning.

We associate conditioning with athletes. We've never watched a professional championship tennis match in which one player was a lean, sinewy six-foot-three-inches tall, and the other stood five-nine, weighed 279 pounds, and needed help from his coach to tie his shoelaces because he couldn't bend over far enough to reach them. That player would never make it to a championship-caliber tournament because part of the game is being quick, agile, and energetic enough to keep hitting hard and running fast even if the match goes several hours.

Other professions demand reasonable conditioning, also. A friend told me about attending a banquet with a newspaper columnist who was married to a well-known surgeon. During the post-meal party, the surgeon drank so much that he passed out. His head hit the table with a loud clunk. People at the table were startled, and their first move was to help him. The columnist, though, said, "Oh no, don't disturb him. Let him rest. He has surgery in the morning."

Would you want to be the one on the table in the morning? Would you want to expose your vital organs to someone with a scalpel and a hangover? This person, regardless of his renowned expertise, had become a liability. If I were the patient, I'd rather wait until he'd had a good night's rest—or at least a potful of coffee.

Writers, too, owe it to their patient—the novel, the magazine article, the screenplay, or whatever project they're working on—to come to the "operating room" well rested and alert.

Conditioning for writers, as for athletes, includes proper nutrition, adequate rest, and reasonable care and maintenance of the mind and body. I'm not qualified to offer specific advice on these. For the purposes of this book, it's sufficient to remind you that fitness may affect your writing. Each of you knows which regimen to follow, which foods to eat, and so on. Be aware of conditioning, and be sensible about it.

Another aspect of conditioning, which again is most apparent in athletes, is attempting to get the most from your body. Athletes try to run faster, throw farther, hit harder, endure longer. Writers can learn from this, also.

Learn when your body works best and then capitalize on that. Is the morning your creative time? Then get up, brush your teeth, have some breakfast, read the paper, and get to the computer. Turn out some magnificent pages, and leave the afternoon for the clerical, noncreative work: paying your bills, updating your records, whatever.

Maybe you're like Bob Hope. He says, "You're only as young as you feel, and I don't feel anything until noon." If you can't get your motor running in the morning, schedule your creative work for the afternoon and evening. Let the mornings be your relaxing time.

One writer I know prefers to work in the middle of the night. It's quiet. The rest of the world doesn't disturb him because it's asleep. Midnight to 5:00 A.M. are his office hours.

Another writing friend of mine couldn't decide on a predictable schedule, so he brought his pressing projects to Las Vegas. Las Vegas is a town that ignores time; there are no clocks in the casinos. This writer goes there so he can complete his assignment without the constraints of time. He writes until he gets hungry. Then, no matter what time of day it is, he can have breakfast . . . or lunch, if he prefers . . . or dinner. He writes until he gets tired. Then, regardless of the time, he can go to sleep.

Discover your best time for working and use it.

Athletes also get the most from their equipment. Baseball players select gloves that have a comfortable feel, gloves that will almost catch the ball for them. They have bats custom-made to their specifications—the right length, weight and feel. Tennis players are finicky about the shoes they wear. Football players must have all parts of their bodies wrapped and taped just so.

Writers should correctly utilize their equipment, too. Is your office chair comfortable? What about your keyboard? Is it the correct height? Is the computer monitor arranged so that you can see it easily, without squinting or scrunching your neck in an awkward position? Do you have adequate lighting and proper ventilation in your work space?

All of these make your workday easier and help improve the quality and quantity of your output.

Finally, athletes pace themselves. They play hard, but they rest when they can. Boxers fight for three minutes each round and rest for one. They take maximum advantage of that rest period. They sit to rest their legs. They drape their arms over the ropes to rest those muscles. They sip water for refreshment. They have someone wave a towel to cool them down. They have an ice-pack on the back of their neck to reenergize their entire body. They cram all the revitalization they can into that short, one-minute span.

Sometimes writers must recognize when they've reached their creative limit. They've exhausted their creative juices and they need to restore that energy. Rather than fight the fatigue, it's good to take that one-minute break between rounds.

Step away from your work for a short period. Take a walk, play a computer game, go see a movie. Do something that will distract you for a brief period. Relax, and then get back to your project. Often you'll find that you're more refreshed, revitalized, and better able to attack your work.

Writing can be a physically and mentally demanding craft. When we keep ourselves in shape, we have a better chance of moving on to the next plateau, of getting our careers moving again at top speed.

CHAPTER 8

HUSBAND YOUR TALENTS

A few years ago I taught at a writing seminar with a fine comedy writer, Bob Orben. Bob wrote for many years for Red Skelton and founded, published and edited a successful and well-respected comedy newsletter, *Current Comedy*. During the seminar's question-and-answer period, one of the students noticed that both Bob and I had receding hairlines and asked, "Do you have to be bald to be a good comedy writer?"

Bob had the ready comeback. He said, "God has given us all only so many hormones. If you want to use yours to grow hair, that's your business."

Some writers may feel that their creative and writing ability is infinite. They're partly right, but they're partly wrong. When I worked on the staff of "The Carol Burnett Show," one of the other writers burst into my office one day and announced in some panic, "Have you heard? All of the funny sketch ideas have been written. There are no more."

We'll never run out of good premises for comedy sketches, intriguing plots for novels, unique angles for nonfiction articles, interesting and educational ideas for children's books, or subjects for poetry. Our creativity is limitless. However, our time and our energy are finite. We only have so much time to devote to our writing, and only so much endurance.

People are naive about creativity. They don't realize that it's work and they refuse to admit that it takes time. "My son has to write a report on the California redwoods. Would you write something up for him? I'd really appreciate it." "Hey, my church choir is trying to get some publicity for our upcoming recital. You're good at writing. Could you write about five or six pieces that would get us in the local papers? I'd really appreciate it."

Even people who should know better don't know better. Many times when I worked on television shows, the star or guest star would poke his head into our office and say, "Gee, I have to go to this big banquet tonight. I know they'll ask me to say something. Could you write something clever for me to say? I only need about twenty minutes. It won't take you any time at all. Thanks."

Once, an associate producer of a show I worked on received a letter from a charitable organization asking our star to write a funny article about the organization. With the star's name on the article, this organization could place it in a major magazine and get some good publicity. The associate producer asked my partner and me to ghostwrite the piece. We did. We received no pay and couldn't write it on company time. The piece we wrote was published in some national periodical and the organization was delighted with it.

A few years later, after the show was off the air, I visited that associate producer's office. Behind his desk, in a place of honor on his wall, was a large plaque from that organization thanking him for his extensive and exhaustive work on behalf of their cause.

Nonwriters are not the least bit embarrassed about asking writers for favors. They have no compunction because writing is not like ditch-digging; it's not really work. (Remember, even my own grandson said about my writing, "He doesn't work. He only types.") The feeling seems to be that we're not donating something of value. Whatever we write, we can always write again.

You as a writer, though, must remember that you are giving away something of value. First, you're giving away time. Like the hormones that Bob Orben spoke of, time is finite. There are only twenty-four hours in a day. Whatever time you spend doing favors or good works for friends, associates or coworkers must be subtracted from your work time. It leaves less that you can devote to furthering your career.

Sometimes the time seems minimal, but there is a cumulative effect. I know a wealthy person who said the same thing about money. People get angry when she refuses to donate even small amounts to their cause. She explained, "People think that I have unlimited wealth. I don't. My fortune is finite. Even if I had $100 million, I would be besieged by a million charities each asking for $100." She donated a reasonable amount to charities she selected and refused all other requests.

This can happen with writers, too. A club you belong to wants you to edit its monthly bulletin. The local school wants you to script the variety show it's putting on as a fund-raiser. People who want to try writing send you manuscripts to read, evaluate and possibly rewrite. You have to budget the amount of time you donate or you won't have enough left to donate to your own progress.

People have another naiveté about writers: They forget that good writers always write well. They'll ask a good writer to write a "lousy" editorial for the local paper; they want him to do a sloppy job of editing the club bulletin; they want him to do a quick and mediocre speech that they can deliver to their annual CPA convention. Good writers can't do that. They would hurt themselves if they did. Good writers must devote time and energy to write and rewrite everything they put on paper. That's why they're good writers.

Each assignment you undertake burns energy. It uses up creativity that you need for your own production. It's like asking a friend to drive you to the airport and to run a few errands for you on the way to and from. Because you do a favor for a friend doesn't mean that your car won't burn gas. The car—and you—use fuel whether you're doing a favor or taking care of business. You can't afford to run out of gas when you're working on your professional assignments.

Don't misunderstand. You don't have to become a curmudgeon and refuse every request for help. You don't want to become the volunteer equivalent of the miser who stuffs all his money in his mattress and refuses to spend even for necessities. Simply be aware that your first duty is to your career and that some of these extracurricular activities, even though they're worthy, can hamper your own writing.

Writing is your job. It's your livelihood, just as standing in front of a class is a teacher's job or spreading mortar and laying bricks is a mason's job. People wouldn't expect a teacher or a bricklayer to take time off from work to do them a favor. But they do sometimes expect writers to take time off from their projects.

Do what you can to help others. What you can't do, refuse.

Remember, too, that you can donate in other areas. You can help Little League by being an umpire; you don't have to do its publicity. You can help the church choir by baking cookies for its social; you don't have to write all of its letters.

Will Rogers was once invited to an affair where the host asked him to stand up and say a few humorous words. Of course, Rogers couldn't refuse, so he did a short monologue. Later, Rogers sent his host a hefty bill for his professional services. The host wrote back and said that the entertainer was not there as a professional performer, but as a guest. Rogers wrote back and said, "When I'm a guest, Mrs. Rogers is usually invited, too."

You only have so much energy and time to devote to your writing. Be sure to use it wisely to get your career moving in high gear.

CHAPTER 9

PROTECT YOUR ENTHUSIASM

I have a black thumb. Any plant I put in my office – and I like living things in the office – dies. Some plants I overwater; others, I underwater. I can give some flowers too much sunshine and others not enough. Whatever I do, the beautiful leaves and petals turn colors nature never intended them to turn, they wilt, and they wistfully wave good-bye to me before dropping sadly to the floor.

I feel guilty. I feel saddened. So much so that I abandon all efforts at raising plants and surrender to plastic and silk flowers in my office.

They died, too.

Living things need care and maintenance to grow properly. They require the correct amount of sunlight, water and nourishment to flourish, stay healthy and grow.

So does creativity. So does a career.

As fragile as those plants were, they were hardy compared to a writer's ego. I have seen authors' enthusiasm shrivel up and die in a matter of seconds when a premise or a project was questioned, even by those who knew nothing about writing. For all of our bluster and bravado, we have about as much confidence as a teenager about to meet his date's parents.

I once worked on a television production that was inundated with notes. Producers, stars, friends of stars – everyone had notes. And we writers had to translate all of those comments into a new working script by morning.

We went through each recommendation page by page, adding dialogue where requested, stronger punch lines where someone thought they were needed, even new scenes if that's what the note dictated. We wrote through dinner, having sent out for sandwiches and soda pops. We wrote and we rewrote, typed and retyped, until at about two in the morning we had only one more joke to write.

The cleaning crew came in and dusted and mopped around us as we tossed ideas back and forth. One more line to go and we could go home, catch a few hours of sleep, and be back for the reading of the new pages at the beginning of the workday. But none of the lines seemed to be working. None seemed better than the original.

Finally, one of the writers threw out an idea that made us all laugh. We said, "That's it. Somebody type it, quick, before we forget it."

Just as someone slipped a sheet of paper into the typewriter and started tapping the keys, the guy who was mopping the floor said, "Don't you think that's reaching a little bit too far for the joke?"

The cleaning guy said this. The janitor. He suggested to five or six highly paid, professional writers that we were "reaching" for a joke. Do you know what we did? That's right. We ripped the page out of the typewriter, crumpled it, and began pacing and tossing ideas again. We worked through the night because someone — anyone — questioned our material.

That's how insecure writers can be about their product. That's dangerous to our passion, our productivity and our progress. Many of us have abandoned projects that we were zealous about simply because someone said a negative word about it. Many worthwhile manuscripts are lost because a friend, relative or passing acquaintance doesn't share our fervor for it.

Shakespeare wrote, "Doubts are traitors and make us lose the good we oft might win by fearing to attempt." He might have been talking to writers. We can have "doubts and fear to attempt" when someone is negative or even indifferent to our work.

Creative people can be a strange combination of emotions. They can be self-assured and daring, while at the same time timid. They can be adventurers who want to forge new paths through uncharted wilderness, while also not wanting to cross the street without permission. They can say, "I'm going to do the Great American Novel the way I want to do it," and follow that two days later with, "Oh, Cousin Martha didn't like chapter one, so I've given up on the novel."

Writing is a difficult profession under the best of circumstances. It's not always easy to be creative. It's especially difficult when we have the Cousin Marthas of the world to confront.

To continue to create and produce, we must protect our delicate insecurities. We must secure our projects in a sterile bubble to keep out the infections of the noncreative world. We must keep our passion glowing at white heat until the project is done, the pages are typed, the creativity has been converted to manuscript.

Here are some suggestions on how to do that.

DON'T LET COUSIN MARTHA READ THE DRAFT

Cousin Martha may be right about chapter one. It may lack drive and direction. And she is certainly entitled to her opinion. Your error was in letting Cousin Martha read chapter one in the first place.

This is an unfinished novel. It's a work in progress. It's your work in progress, and no one else is qualified to judge it yet— especially not Martha.

Can you imagine someone sitting in Michelangelo's studio as he is about to begin work on a new piece of marble? The master takes his hammer and chisel and chips away at the block. After five or six strokes, the visitor says, "I don't know, Mike, somehow it doesn't seem to look like anything yet." This critic would wind up with a chisel in his ear.

That's why artists cover their unfinished canvases with a cloth. They don't want others' opinions. This is *their* work. They have a concept in mind, and no one can know what that concept is until it is completed. Only then can another person evaluate the work.

Just as no one can criticize an artist's brushstrokes until they are all on the canvas, so no one can appraise your writing until the writing is done. Even if your beloved cousin is correct about chapter one, the chances are you would have noticed it and re-written it. Nothing is written until it is rewritten. In that sense there is nothing for Cousin Martha to judge. There is no chapter one yet; there is only a first draft of chapter one.

The danger is that the negative thoughts may deter you from rewriting the chapter. They may prompt you to postpone this project or abandon it altogether. Many of us writers are that insecure.

In fact, it's the insecurity that causes us to show the pages in the first place. We want reinforcement. We want corroboration that our work is worthwhile. Either that, or we're just fishing for glorious compliments. That's unnecessary. You're the artist; you're the one with the idea. You know when it works and when it doesn't. At least, you know a lot more about it than your cousin.

You, the writer, must be bold enough to forge ahead with your premise, flesh it out, get it on paper, and then have the courage to let people read and evaluate it. Isn't that what all writers do?

Suppose you say, though, that you need some competent help with this project. Okay. That's different. Give it to qualified critics for their opinions, their suggestions, their ideas. If they're competent and qualified, they'll realize that they're dealing with a work in progress. They'll also realize that they're dealing with a frightened artist who has to be treated delicately.

And if you are determined to seek opinions before your manuscript is completed, prepare yourself for a few negatives. Make sure that you're strong enough to take criticism and still continue with this project. If you're not, then you're risking this idea totally. Is it worth it?

CONSIDER THE SOURCE

I've written for several years for the Bob Hope television specials. I'm always amused by television people I meet at parties who tell me, "Here's what I think Bob Hope has been doing wrong. . . ."

Bob Hope has compiled an unparalleled record in show business. He was a top attraction in vaudeville, a major star on Broadway, at the top of the ratings in radio, a number-one box-office draw in films, and his television ratings are incredible. He's been on television for more than forty years, his shows have continuously been in the top ten, and many of the highest-rated specials of all time are Bob Hope specials. Yet these neophytes know what Bob Hope and his staff have been doing wrong.

When you are known as a writer, you'll be bombarded with all sorts of recommendations, suggestions and advice. Your duty is to separate the precious from the useless, the worthwhile from the worthless. Everyone is entitled to her opinion, but not everyone has earned the right to have her opinion heeded.

Some comedian—it might have been George Burns—once said that the problem with the world today is that all the people who know how to run it are driving taxicabs.

How do we evaluate the worth of suggestions we receive, whether solicited or unsolicited? The tendency is to listen to those who agree with us and dismiss those who don't. Obviously, that won't speed our progress.

Consider two things when evaluating advice: Does the person offering it know what she is talking about? Does that person have something at stake?

Let's go back to Bob Hope and his critic. Suppose you could turn the clock back and begin Mr. Hope's career at point zero. If you had it to do all over again, would you do what Mr. Hope chose to do, or what this advice-giver suggests? I think you'd choose Mr. Hope's ideas. Why? Because they've been proven successful. This person has been there. He knows where the pitfalls are and how to avoid them. He's been in the fray. He's been victorious. He knows what he's talking about.

If the person offering you suggestions has been a publisher for many years, a distinguished editor, a novelist, a journalist or a poet, perhaps you should pay attention to his recommendations. At least consider them. They might help.

If the person knows nothing about the business, don't allow that criticism to affect you or your work. Don't permit it to kill your enthusiasm. If something that person says seems to have merit, heed it; if it doesn't, dismiss it. You know more about writing than he does.

Second, consider if your advisor has something at stake. If not, the advice has to be suspect. It's easy for someone to say, "If Arnold Schwarzenegger refused to give me an autograph, I'd punch him right in the nose." However, if he came face to face with "The Terminator" and realized how massive and powerful he is, he'd think twice about throwing the first punch. He'd realize quickly that perhaps his actions should be reconsidered.

Don't put too much stock in any suggestions that are offered by people who won't have to face the consequences. They can offer the advice, but you're the one who will have to deal with the results. So be careful.

AVOID NEGATIVE PEOPLE

Most of the writing assignments I get are delivered by phone. When Person A calls, she's full of enthusiasm. The assignment thrills her, and she transfers that excitement about the project to me. Consequently, I attack my writing with gusto and produce worthwhile results quickly.

When Person B calls, he's depressing. He doesn't like the assignment, doesn't think it's inventive, and conveys that to me on the phone. I begin my writing with a defeatist's attitude. The writing is sluggish. I'm not intrigued by the project, and my work is not inspired. It takes me forever to write abnormally mediocre material.

The difference is in the caller. If Person A called with the other assignment, I would be eager to do it and would work better and faster. I know because sometimes when I'm stalled, I call Person A and discuss the assignment. Her energy picks me up, and my writing improves immediately.

Negative people are contagious. They spread the disease. Negativity is a blight for writers. It not only affects our work, but also our careers. I work with beginning writers and find that many approach their careers with a negative attitude. "No publisher will ever look at my work." "I've just written a short story, but I don't think it's any good." These become self-fulfilling prophecies. Also, that thinking affects that person's writing. Why sweat over the rewrite of a manuscript when you sincerely believe that no publisher will look at it?

You can spot negativity in your associates. Know that it's deadly to your own enthusiasm. Either avoid those people, or learn to disregard their comments.

MAINTAIN A CREATIVE ATMOSPHERE

As television producers, my partner and I had one firm rule that we explained to the writing staff at the beginning of each session: We would maintain a creative atmosphere in the writing offices.

That meant that all ideas would be voiced freely and openly, without fear of being ridiculed. We wanted the input of the entire staff and we knew that making fun of some of the writers would silence them. They would keep their ideas to themselves.

This doesn't mean we accepted all ideas that were voiced. If they were no good, we said they were no good. But we, and the entire staff, would say it in a professional, considerate way—a way that encouraged further ideas.

You, too, should create a positive, creative atmosphere in your workplace. This can take any form you like. It might involve the color of your walls. It might involve cheery knick-knacks around the office. It could be photos of your professional idols. Or it might be an answering machine turned on during your most productive hours so that you don't have to deal with distracting, disturbing phone calls.

Creative ambience is important. In most offices I visit, I see posters and photos of the occupant in all of her glory. Rarely do they display reminders of their failures. They want to be inspired to do their best work, so they remind themselves of it.

You know best what will bring out your creativity. Surround yourself with it.

HAVE FAITH IN YOUR WORK

Television writers must endure the ordeal of "pitching." Pitching is when you face the buyers one-on-one and "talk down" your story idea. You have to *sell* your story.

A former partner of mine said that the greatest friend a writer could have at these pitch sessions was a cigar — a big cigar. Why? Because it generated courage.

A timid writer might go in and say, "I have a story — well it's not really a story yet, it's just an idea — but it's a story about a girl who works in an office. She has some friends, you know, they're kind of interesting, and I think fascinating — well, I hope fascinating — things happen to them . . . " and the pitch session continues this way. No spark, no fire.

My partner says that if you give that writer a cigar, he becomes a tiger. He says, "I have the greatest idea in the history of writing. I'm telling you that this is about a fascinating woman who goes to work in the most interesting office in the world." All the time he's waving his cigar. He goes on, "And she has friends, but not just any friends. These are interesting, entertaining, witty friends. And they get into the most captivating situations you ever heard of. . . . " With the cigar, this writer sells.

There's a soupçon of truth to that, but the point I'm making is that something — in this case, the cigar — gave that writer courage and faith in the idea. That's what made the difference, not the stogie.

You must find a way to generate that same belief in your work. Probably the best way is good, solid preparation. Do your homework well. Know that your manuscript is good. Know that you've done extensive research and written and rewritten your project to the best of your ability. That'll do more for your self-image than any two-dollar cigar will.

Your enthusiasm is an indispensable tool in your writing. Guard it fiercely. One suggestion is to write your novel, sell it, and have it make the bestseller list. Do that, and then you won't give a good hoot or a holler whether Cousin Martha likes the first chapter or not.

CHAPTER 10

TAKE SOME RISKS

Perhaps you've heard of the world-famous diver who would leap off a platform 150 feet high into a wading pool filled with only 1 foot of water. People couldn't believe such a feat was possible and would pack the stadium for each performance.

The diver would come out and wave to the cheering crowd, toss off his sequined cape, and climb the ladder slowly but bravely. Each step would draw murmurs from the crowd and loud "oohs" and "aahs." The ladder was so tall and slender that it would shimmy in the breeze. Just climbing it was a stunt that awed the spectators.

Finally, he would stand on the small platform 150 feet in the air and stare down at the tiny target of water below. The crowd would be silent. Then, holding onto the ladder behind him with one hand, he would raise the other hand in address to the crowd. He would say, "Ladies and gentlemen, what I'm about to do is impossible." People in the audience would turn and nod to one another, then immediately turn back to hear what else this daredevil had to say.

He'd continue: "I have a lovely, devoted wife and three beautiful, young children who adore me and depend on me for their livelihood. How many of you have children at home?" Some would raise their hands, others would applaud in answer to his question.

"If I dive off of this platform I will surely be severely injured, permanently disabled or perhaps worse." The audience would agree and begin to feel guilty that they wanted to watch this disaster.

The daredevil went on: "Do you want me to do that, ladies and gentlemen? Do you want me to dive? Do you want that on your conscience?"

The compassionate crowd would shout, "No! No! Don't jump!"

The diver would bow resignedly to their wishes, then stand erect again and say, "Thank you, my good people, thank you. And remember, the next performances are at 5:00 and 7:00 tonight. Bring your friends."

Then he would climb down the ladder.

Of course, it's only a joke, but it illustrates a point. This guy was pulling a scam. He was deceiving his audience. He never had any intention of diving into that shallow pool.

Climbing up the ladder was easy. Giving the impression that he was a fearless, death-defying diver was easy. For him, conning the audience was easy. Only the diving would have been difficult.

Sometimes we writers are like that daredevil. We go through the motions of wanting to progress to the next writing plateau. We exhibit all the bravado and bluster of wanting to further our careers. But like the character in our tale, we have no intention of progressing. We may not be totally satisfied with our present level of achievement, but we're comfortable with it. We know the heartaches involved and we've learned to handle them. Staying where we are is safer than facing new challenges.

The reluctant diver in the anecdote fooled his audience. Sometimes we writers fool ourselves, too. We're never sure what hazards lurk on the next plateau. Can we handle them? Will they attack and fling us back a few plateaus? We don't know. So we choose to stay where we are and not tempt the monsters of the next level of achievement.

It seems prudent. Even military strategists advise against foolhardy courage. It's wiser, they say, to "live to fight another day." But being afraid to progress is not fighting some other day; it's total surrender. It's saying, "I've progressed far enough. I don't want to risk my present success. I'm comfortable where I am."

The problem is that we don't gain much without jeopardy.

Even the comfortable success we now enjoy was bought at some risk. You probably drive a car. You get into it with no fear or hesitation, you'll venture onto any highway with confidence. You'll go anywhere in your trusty Chevy, Toyota or whatever you drive. But think back to when you first learned how to drive. Your dad may have taught you. Perhaps a friend. Maybe you learned in driver's ed in school. However you learned, you were probably terrified your first time behind the wheel. You hesitated when your instructor said, "Turn the key." Your fingers paused while your mind mentally weighed the percentages. Was it worth the risk of starting this vehicle with *you* in the driver's seat?

Then you were told to shift the car into gear. You did — slowly. Your instructor told you to step on the gas. You did — carefully. Then you were driving, but not steering boldly at all.

You were genuinely frightened. In your mind, you were taking considerable risk. Today, though, all of that fear is gone and you drive without even realizing it at times. You handle that car as if it were paid for. You wouldn't be driving today, though, unless you worked your way through that fear, unless you took a chance and tried driving a car.

Your career might be stalled because of an intimidation — probably an unfounded intimidation — of the next level. The solution is to get a little more daring, more aggressive. Take a few chances.

First, take some risks with your writing. It's good for novice writers to follow the traditional rules. Those rules are traditional because they work. They're good advice. Following them helps a writer to build a solid technical foundation and to get established in the business. However, those rules can become monotonous. They can inhibit your literary pioneering spirit. Besides, it's inviting and exhilarating to break rules every once in a while. So do it.

As the old cowboy saying advises: "There ain't no horse that's never been rode, and ain't no cowboy that's never been throwed." You can end a sentence with a preposition if you want to. You can misspell words if it feels natural for your character. "Cain't nobody find no fawlt with that." You can even misspell some in your own voice if it gives your writing oomph. I remember a movie that was narrated by a person who was killed in the opening scene. That's normally against the rules. But in 1950, Charles Brackett, Billy Wilder and D.M. Marshman, Jr. won an Academy Award for writing that screenplay. It was called *Sunset Boulevard*.

Don't misunderstand; this is not a license to break rules promiscuously. There's no gain in breaking rules just to break them. But there's no sense, either, in being afraid to break a rule when you feel that might add some luster to your writing.

What can happen if you transgress? Well, you can find it opens new trails for you as a writer, or you can discover that you shouldn't break that particular rule again. That's all. In either case, you'll probably find that your "naughtiness" was an adventure. It might put a little verve into your writing and some fire into you.

The second area for you to get more daring in is your marketing. Explore markets that you've shied away from. The worst they can do is add to your collection of polite rejection notices. The best that can happen is that one or more of these markets will like your style and purchase some of your writing. You'll wind up with a prestigious, higher-paying client, and you'll boost your career a notch.

Be uncomfortable with your comfortable niche in the writing world. Take some chances. Get more daring.

This is not to suggest that you become suicidal in your headlong rush into uncharted literary territory. There's a difference between being aggressive and being reckless. Certainly you should exercise prudence in any new undertaking, but it can be discreetly combined with some adventure.

A writing friend of mine had a cozy list of clients that he sold to regularly. This provided an income that he was not unhappy with. However, he was unhappy with his progress. He sold consistently and he sold often to the midlist markets, yet he felt he was not reaching his full potential as a writer.

Despite his dissatisfaction, he wouldn't approach the better markets. Why? Because they intimidated him. He suffered from the "Oh, they won't buy from me" syndrome.

When he worked up the courage, though, to approach those markets, they welcomed his material. They purchased his material — even more than the midlist markets did.

This writer didn't leave his regular markets until the better ones replaced them. He didn't abandon his regular clients; he outgrew them. He progressed at a quick, but reasonable, pace. He moved on to the next level of his career simply because he worked up the courage to take a chance and approach that next level.

You can take a few judicious chances and try to move your career into high gear, or you can be the writing equivalent of the diving daredevil who opened this chapter.

"Ladies and gentlemen," you shout, "I am about to attempt to write the Great American Novel." You hear a roar of approval from the crowd.

"However, should I fail, I will be destroyed by the critics, ridiculed by my family and friends, banished by responsible publishers, and perhaps ruined professionally." The audience is hushed.

"Do you want me to do that, ladies and gentlemen? Do you want that on your conscience?" You hear the world shout, "No! No!"

You say, "Thank you, good people. Thank you. I shall begin my next Great American Novel around September. Tell your friends about it."

PART II

LOOK TO YOUR WRITING

"I was working on the proof of one
of my poems all the morning, and took out
a comma. In the afternoon
I put it back again."

OSCAR WILDE

CHAPTER 11

RETURN TO BASICS

Basics are geeky. They're boring. They're annoying. They're inhibiting. They keep us from getting into the real fun. You want to study piano so you can play like Elton John. Instead, the teacher has you sitting up straight with your hands just so, your fingers positioned precisely over the keys. You don't play Elton John tunes; you play "I Am Mr. Middle C." Boring.

You sign up for golf lessons because you want to go out with your foursome next weekend and hit shots like you saw the masters make when you watched the PGA championship on television. You bite the bullet and pay the money because you think the skills you learn and the money you win from your unsuspecting partners will be worth it. Then the instructor says, "I think we'd better work on your grip." You think, "Man, I didn't fork over fifty bucks to change my grip. I want to hit the ball 338 yards off the tee. I want to set it on the green with bite and backspin. I want to putt from 40 feet and drop it into the cup." Your instructor says, "Move your thumb about a quarter inch to the right." Boring.

As a producer for situation comedies, I would meet with freelance writers, listen to them pitch their story ideas, then decide whether to buy one of their ideas. When I bought, they were delighted — for a little while.

Immediately following the acceptance, I would say to them, "When can you have an outline ready for me?" Now, most of these writers had an extensive list of credits. Quite a few had written as many, or more, shows than I had. They resented having to submit something as basic as an outline.

"I don't usually work from an outline," one writer said.

"You do now," I said.

I required an outline because it was basic. It served as a written record of what I had purchased. It also gave me and my staff an opportunity to review the complete plot. We could discuss and correct any errors before the writers finalized it in script form.

I felt it helped the writers, too. It was a documentation of what we discussed in the meeting. If there were any misunderstandings, they could be corrected before the more serious writing began. It also forced them to think through the entire story before beginning it. Television writers are prone to "blue sky" — that is, talking in such broad terms that there's no real substance. Reducing the story to an outline eliminates most of that problem.

Once my writing partner and I blue skied an idea to the producers of a show called "Joe and Sons." They bought our premise, but we had such a tight deadline that we couldn't present an outline. We had to get the show written quickly. We worked on the script and painted ourselves into a corner. We had created such an intriguing dilemma that we couldn't find a resolution to it. We had no idea how our show would end. Eventually, the producers called and said the show was canceled. "Turn in what you have so far and you'll be paid for the complete script," they said. We did.

To this day we have no idea how that show would have ended. Preparing an outline would have forced us to find an ending before starting to write.

The outline also helps writers stay within the time confines of television. Each situation comedy is only one-half hour; therefore, each act and scene is limited by fairly rigid time constraints. For instance, you can't have Act One, Scene One run for twenty-four minutes and then allow the rest of the play only six minutes. By having a detailed outline, the writers know what must be accomplished by a certain page number. It keeps the teleplay well balanced.

Basics can be boring, geeky; but they do serve a purpose.

Another strange thing about basics is that they're touted by instructors, but not always practiced by them. I had a guitar teacher once who insisted on rigidly correct posture. My right foot had to be planted firmly on the floor while my left perched on the classical guitar footrest. The instrument had to rest affectionately on my left knee, while I sat in a hard chair with my back straight. My right hand had to be arched over the strings with the thumb projecting along the fingerboard. My left thumb was never permitted to sneak more than halfway up the back of the neck. When it would, my instructor would push it back down. Those were his rules, and he enforced them like a musical policeman.

They were not only irritating; they were uncomfortable.

Then I went to see my teacher play in a jazz club. He was so slouched over it looked like he left his spine at home. The guitar was stuck in his middle like a crutch to keep him from sliding off the chair. His hands were limp, and a cigarette dangling from his mouth as he played forced him to keep one eye semiclosed as protection from the rising, acrid smoke. But he played beautifully.

I wondered, though, if he played like this, why he forced me to play with such military posture. I came up with these answers: First, he was an accomplished guitarist; I wasn't. He had already worked through the basics; I hadn't. He had strengthened and stretched his fingers with years of rudimentary exercises; I hadn't. He'd practiced and rehearsed and knew exactly what he had to do to play these tunes he was performing in this club. He had earned the right to take liberties, and knew the price he would pay for taking them. I hadn't earned the right to cut corners. Second, he'd proven himself. He had the gig. He'd been hired to play in this club. I wasn't good enough to play with a jazz combo, so I couldn't relax my technique. I couldn't rest on my laurels because I had no laurels to rest on. Third, even though my instructor played beautifully with this group, I wondered how much better he might have sounded and how much more respected he would have been as a musician if he had followed his own regulations. There's no way of knowing.

However, I did get a chance to see the master classical guitarist, Segovia, in concert. I also saw Christopher Parkening, one of his students, play. They both sat exactly as my instructor had taught me to sit.

Nevertheless, the questions remain: How important are basics for relative beginners? Can they later be abandoned or ignored—or outgrown? Is it beneficial for an artist to periodically return to fundamentals?

BASICS FOR BEGINNERS

Fundamentals serve various purposes for the beginner. They provide a firm foundation on which to build your education and your skills. For instance, in studying music, the student learns to practice the scales. But while she learns how to move her fingers over the keyboard, she also learns the formulas on which all music is structured. The simple do-re-mi of the scales and the relationship that each note within that scale has with the others is solid musical theory. Learning that concept builds the foundation from which more complex principles can be learned.

In working with beginning comedy writers, I insist that they begin their writing on any given topic by first making a list of references to that topic. For example, if they were to write about the weather, they would begin by creating a list of weather references, such as "high pressure, low pressure, warm mass of air, barometer reading, forecast, partly cloudy, partly sunny, smoggy, hazy, rain, snow, sleet. . . . " The list must consist of fifty or more items.

I suggest this because most jokes are two or more references tied together in a unique way. For example, "We've had so much wet weather in California that the forecast is rain all day today followed by a 50 percent chance of tomorrow." This gag combines the meteorologist's jargon with the threat of being washed away.

If beginners learn to assemble a good compilation of references, they give themselves plenty of ammunition to write their jokes. They also learn the rhythm and structure of the gags.

The basics, too, allow us to gradually build skills as we learn our craft. A young music student not only learns the scales when he plays them; he also stretches and limbers up his fingers, which helps with technique. Comedian Jack Benny used to kid about his violin playing, but he loved the instrument, had studied it as a youngster, and practiced devoutly as an adult. He played with many symphonies and with some great masters. One of these violin virtuosos once said that Mr. Benny was a good player, but he would never become a great player. Regardless of how much he practiced and studied as an adult, his fingers had never acquired the dexterity that extraordinary musicianship requires. He hadn't practiced the fundamentals seriously enough at an early age.

The comedy-writing students who compile a list of references acquire a facility in finding these references. Gradually, they learn to search out these references mentally, without the need of a formal, written list.

That's another thing that learning the fundamentals does for us: It allows us to make certain necessary moves automatic. Again, if you watch a professional guitarist, you'll notice that her fingers glide over the complicated fingerboard with ease. She never has to look down to be sure that she's on the right fret; she just does it. Why? Because she's practiced those basics until they became second nature to her.

I see this happen with the beginning comedy writers I work with. As they follow the rules strictly in the beginning—writing out lists, doing everything step by step—they gain a feel for the rhythm and structure of the joke form. With practice, that then becomes so familiar to them that the elements of the gags fall into place more easily and their writing becomes faster and better.

The basics also allow us to build confidence in our skills. Despite all my talk of guitar playing and study, I'm not a musician. If someone asks me to play, I break out in a cold sweat and my fingers go brain-dead. They don't remember where they should be or what they should be doing. Accomplished guitarists, though, play very easily. They know they can razzle-dazzle most audiences with just a few simple chords and maybe a fundamental melody line. They know the basics, and that's enough to please most listeners.

People often ask me if I ever suffer from writer's block. They wonder if there is ever a time when I can't think of a joke to write. I've discussed this with the other writers on the Bob Hope staff and we all admit that it never happens. There is no topic that we can't write about.

Why? Because we have confidence in the basics that allow us to write our jokes. Every topic, regardless of how obscure, has references. With those references, we can find combinations that sound funny. We can write jokes.

WHEN BASICS BECOME REFLEXIVE

In a sense, you don't graduate from the basics so much as you absorb them. You learn them so well that they become a part of everything you do. You can't unlearn them.

Most of the fundamentals you acquire become reflexive. They can't be abandoned, ignored or outgrown. As you type, for example, you don't think about your fingers or where the letters are; you simply type.

Some basic rules, though, are not so automatic. For example, your typing instructor surely taught you that it was wise to sit up straight when typing. Not all of us do that. We relax that rule. We recognize the wisdom of it, but we grant ourselves dispensations, for whatever reasons.

In the example I gave earlier, my guitar instructor ignored his own regulations about posture. He taught his students to sit correctly, but he didn't practice what he preached.

Does it hurt to abandon some of this learning? Yes and no. Often, it does no harm. If you have a simple paragraph to type, you can do it from a slouched position, a kneeling position — even prostrate, if you like. Your fingers will still find the right keys and you'll suffer no ill effects. However, if you have to type for eight hours a day, five days a week, you'll want a comfortable chair. You'll want to maintain a posture that will have the least wear and tear on your back. That posture is probably the one your first typing teacher taught you.

Some professionals can ignore the basics if the project they're working on is simple. Someone who knows how to play the classics on the piano can play "I Am Mr. Middle C" without assuming the correct position over the keyboard. He can sit any way he wants and play that simple ditty well. However, if he is to play a complex classical concerto, he'll want to do some finger exercises, warm up a bit and sit properly before the piano. This piece, he knows, requires skill, dexterity and concentration. He'll want all of his training available for this performance.

In my own comedy writing, I rarely make a written list of references before beginning my work. I usually don't need one. However, when my work gets tired or predictable, I make a written list. I want better references; I want better jokes. I go back to the basics.

Fundamentals—both the automatic and the nonautomatic—are always important. It's foolhardy to think that we've ever progressed to the point where we've outgrown them.

GETTING BACK TO BASICS

If you want to shift your career into high gear and get it moving with more verve, the first place you should look is to the basics. They're constructive for several reasons.

First, basics are called basics because they're—well—basic. They're the foundation on which all else is built. There was a joke going around a few years ago about a man who would periodically get up, go to his window and shout outside, "Green side up. Green side up." After he did this several times, his wife asked, "What are you doing?" The man said, "I hired the dumbest gardeners in the world and I have to keep reminding them how to lay the new sod."

It's a nonsensical joke, but it illustrates that if you get the fundamentals wrong, everything after that will be wrong. If you're going to lay sod, you really do want the green side up.

Everything is built on basics. A flaw in the fundamentals will taint every step that follows, whether those steps are performed correctly or not. My tennis-instructor friend, Vic Braden, reduces his tennis instructions to the basics. Students ask, "Why did my ball fly over the fence?" Vic says, "Because you hit it there." Another asks, "Why did my shot go into the bottom of the net?" Vic says, "Because you hit it there."

Tennis, he explains, is very simple. The ball is round; it will go wherever you and your racquet aim it. That's basic.

When you hit a writing slump and you don't know why, stop and review the fundamentals. Be sure you're doing what you were taught, as you were taught. Getting yourself and your writing back on firm, solid, fundamental footing can help eliminate errors you didn't even think you were making.

Keep laying the sod green side up.

The second way basics are constructive is that they're the quickest and easiest way to correct faults. I'm always amazed when I watch sporting events and listen to the expert analysts. They can spot flaws instantly that I can't even see after six and seven slow-motion replays. The flaws they spot are usually minute details.

A pitcher is getting bombarded by the opposing team. They're clobbering him for long ball after long ball. He can't get his control. The analyst says, "He's dropping his pitching arm too far." Then he shows it on slow motion and eventually you can see what he's talking about. The pitcher is forgetting one of the basic rules.

A basketball player is missing his foul shots. The analyst says, "He has to bend his knees more." It's basic.

It applies to almost every skill. Flaws are usually traceable back to the basics. Rather than spend hours and hours of detective work trying to find out how a flaw crept into your technique, why not review the basics? Be sure they're proper, and that will probably correct the fault.

Third, going back to solid fundamentals helps eliminate any sloppiness or laziness that you've allowed to creep into your craft. Some of us get a little cocky. We feel that we've outgrown the rudiments of our profession. We can get a little slipshod in our performance.

Good basic technique will eliminate that almost immediately. It's impossible to sit up correctly before the typewriter and slouch at the same time. It just can't be done.

There are basics in all forms of writing. Going into the fundamentals of each writing genre would be too extensive for this book. Instead, let me illustrate how going back to the basics helps my writing.

I write many monologues on various topics. When I was a beginning comedy writer, serving a self-imposed apprenticeship, I followed a strict prewriting regimen. I read newspaper reports about my topic, underlining salient points. Then I would gather a list of references. These would be words, phrases, people, places—practically anything that might be related to my topic. Then I would divide my main topic into subtopics. For instance, if I were writing about how hot the weather was, I would divide that into the following subtopics:

a. General topic (how hot is it?)
b. How the heat made me feel
c. How it affected others (my family, my pets, etc.)
d. What it was doing to things (killing my plants, making the car hot, burning the paint off my house, etc.)
e. Ways to avoid the heat
f. Some good things that the heat spell has accomplished

With all that preparatory work completed, I would begin to write my jokes for the monologue.

Today, I don't always have the time or the luxury of doing this preparatory work. Often the jokes have to be done on the spot. The comic will say, "I have to go onstage now. Give me some opening lines about this auditorium." Consequently, I get a little sloppy.

However, when I notice that my work is becoming predictable, or when I find that I can't work as quickly as I want to, it's because I'm neglecting these basics. As soon as I revert to them, the quantity and quality of my joke writing improves.

Whatever writing you do, recall what you were taught as a beginner. When you hit a slump, return to those fundamentals.

The basics still have value and impact, regardless of how far your career has advanced. If your career has stalled or is not moving at the pace you prefer, and you suspect your writing, turn to the basics. Recheck them; correct them. That will eliminate many faults—some you're aware of and possibly a few you're not. It should help you get your career shifted into high gear.

CHAPTER 12

GET MORE EDUCATION

Once I visited a streetside art show in New York City. One artist's work fascinated me and I studied several of his pieces. The artist, sensing a sale, gave me some history about each piece I studied. I asked how much one small painting was, and he seemed hesitant to give me a price.

"How much do you want to pay for it?" he asked.

I said, "Well, I want to pay whatever the price is."

He said, "Well, give me whatever you think it's worth."

I really had no idea what it was worth and I told him so. I didn't know if he was famous. I doubted it, but I wasn't sure. I didn't really know if he was any good or not. I enjoy art, but I don't know much about it.

He said, "Well, I'm just so happy that you want to buy something of mine that I don't know what to charge."

Somehow we arrived at a fair (I guess) price and I purchased the small painting, but now I was more intrigued by the artist than by his work.

I said, "Don't you sell much?"

He said, "No."

I asked why.

He said, "I don't know. I don't think I've really found my style yet."

"But you've got all these paintings on display?"

He said, "Oh yes, I paint a lot because I love to paint, but I'm not yet painting what I feel."

"Why don't you paint what you feel?" It seemed to be the next natural question.

"I don't know," he confessed. "I know kind of what I want to do, but I don't yet know how to do it. I don't have the brushstrokes, or the right color mixes, or the feel on the canvas."

I felt sad for him, and glad I bought a painting. I said, "Where do you study?"

He said, "Oh, I don't study. I don't want to destroy what I already have."

He had just admitted to me that he had practically nothing—little recognition by the art community, minimal sales, not enough technical skill to convert his ideas to canvas—yet he didn't want to jeopardize that.

Some of us writers are like that struggling artist. We prefer the status quo to more knowledge. Why? Are we, like the artist, afraid of losing what we've got? There's little chance of that. The more we learn about our craft, the more we appreciate our own talent, or the more we recognize the deficiencies in our own skills. Either way, that's good. If we have deficiencies (and I guarantee we all do), education can help us not only recognize them, but also begin to correct them.

Sometimes we probably shy away from education because we're afraid it will uncover our weaknesses. "I don't want to study under that teacher. She might see that I'm not as good as I think I am." Someone once said, "It's better to be quiet and thought a fool than to open your mouth and remove all doubt." Writers sometimes feel that putting their words on paper will "remove all doubt" about their talent.

A *little* knowledge can be a dangerous thing when it convinces us that it's a *lot* of knowledge.

My former writing partner taught me the value of continuing education. It had nothing to do with writing; it had to do with guitar-playing. I love guitar and am a self-taught guitarist. Well, I'm almost self-taught. When I was in high school a friend taught me a few basic chords. I learned C, F and G7. With those few chords he and I could play for hours while our friends sang along around the campfire. We could play practically any song with those three chords. However, we could only play in the key of C major.

I got to be pretty proficient at switching my fingers from chord to chord and strumming the rhythm on the guitar. I also began to develop an ear for the music, knowing almost instinctively when to change from C to G7 or to F. And the others in school loved to sing along with us.

However, if they wanted to join the chorus, they had three choices: sing with us in the key of C, keep their mouths shut or sing off-key. The way we played and sang, it didn't matter much which one they chose.

Later, I bought books of music where not all of the songs were written in the key of C, but that was all right. If it had another chord listed, I would learn that chord and play it.

My writing partner had been a professional musician in the big-band era. He had played with most of the well-known bands and later with many of the top vocalists in nightclubs and recordings. He advised me to take a course in music theory.

I didn't understand why I should. I could play almost any song if I had the music in front of me. What more did I need to know? But he persisted. "Study music," he said, "and see if you aren't astounded by what you learn."

I did, and I was.

There was a mathematical formula to music, a logic to it. It was amazing. There was a relationship between one key and another. There was an actual, honest-to-goodness theory to music. It had been there since Bach and Handel and Mozart. Beethoven had used the same rules to compose his melodic concertos as Willie Nelson used to create his toe-tapping songs.

What was astounding, though, was how this discovery opened up music for me. Now that I knew the "why" of music, I could use that to learn the "how." I no longer had to play just what was written. I could experiment, substitute, improvise. I knew why one key was related to another, so I learned how to transpose from one key to another.

Just this smidgeon of musical education made the guitar

much more fun for me. I could play along with the radio and recordings. I could pick up a favorite country-and-western album and do some fancy picking along with Willie and Waylon and the boys.

It didn't necessarily make me a lot better—that would have to come with more practice—but it made music more understandable for me. It opened up more avenues in music for me to try, to explore. It made music more fun.

It also helped me appreciate how fascinating the study of music is. Anyone who thinks she knows it all about any subject doesn't know how much there is to that subject. That's the saddest kind of ignorance there is.

Continuing your education can benefit your writing career in many ways.

Knowledge of your profession or your particular writing specialty gives an overall concept to it, a dimension, a relationship of one thing to another. For example, suppose a friend gives you directions to his house. He lives in Garborville; you have no idea where that is.

Nevertheless, his directions are explicit and complete. "Take Interstate 22 north until you hit the Main Street exit. Go right off the exit until you hit Fourteenth Avenue. You'll recognize it because there's a big red store on the corner. Turn left on Fourteenth and continue on until you see the sign that says Garborville, Route 57. Turn left at that street. Stay on 57 until you hit Elm Street. Turn right on Elm and then turn right at the very next street. Stay on that until you can't go any farther, then turn right. At the next street, Fairley Road, turn right again, and we're the third house from the corner—537 Fairley Road."

Those directions, if followed absolutely, will get you to your friend's house. However, you still have no idea of where you're going. You know you're headed north because Interstate 22 north probably goes in that direction, but you don't know how far north. Is the Main Street exit five miles down the road? Ten miles? Twenty-five miles? You don't know.

What will you do if you go three or four exits and see a sign that says, "Main Street—Brighton, next exit"? Should you take the Main Street—Brighton exit or continue on until you come to a sign that simply says "Main Street"? You're not sure, are you?

Now how far do you travel on Main Street until you hit Fourteenth Avenue? If you've traveled fifteen miles without seeing Fourteenth Avenue, should you worry that you missed it? Or do you still have another five miles to go? You have no way of knowing.

You have this same dilemma at almost every crucial turn-off along the way. These instructions are accurate, but there's no dimension to them, there's no relationship.

If, however, you get out a map to check these directions, you'll have an overall concept of where you're going and how far each leg of the journey is. Now you can follow your friend's directions and feel confident you're going in the right direction.

That's what education can do for your writing. It can provide that road map so you can corroborate your efforts. Is your screenplay in the right format? Is it the right length? Does it follow the accepted rules? Check it against what you've learned.

What about your novel? Are the characters developed sufficiently? Is there enough intrigue in your plot? Check it against what you've learned.

Are you querying publishers properly? Is your lead paragraph compelling enough? Check it against what you've learned.

This additional education not only gives you direction, but it also lends confidence to your journey. You feel comfortable that you haven't gone astray, which can help you zoom along at a faster pace.

For those, like the streetside artist, who are afraid that education may destroy what they already have: Baloney. A map doesn't destroy the directions you have; it complements them. I can't think of any knowledge that would destroy whatever education went before it. Being able to play the classics on the piano doesn't mean being *un*able to sit at the keyboard and play "Found a Peanut."

Knowledge can also open up other interesting avenues for you to explore. Let's go back to the road map example again.

When you check your friend's directions on the map, you may see a quicker, more direct route, or one that you know better and feel more comfortable with. You're free to take that and save yourself some time and concern.

Knowing more about writing can open up new avenues for you to explore, also. You may discover new genres that intrigue you, or new devices to help with your present writing.

A writing colleague of mine was afraid of new technology. He used an electric typewriter because that's all his office had, but he resented it. He had learned to compose on a manual, and he preferred to compose on a manual. Fewer things went wrong with them. If he accidentally brushed a key, it wouldn't automatically type something onto the paper. Sure, electrics were faster, but speed wasn't everything in writing creatively.

Computers he wouldn't even touch. Not only were they beyond his intelligence; they were downright satanic. He readily admitted that he could hardly work a toaster properly, so how could he ever hope to master a computer?

Another mutual friend, a Scrabble opponent, bought this guy an electronic Scrabble game for his birthday. He loved it. He struggled through the instructions and became a semiaddict, playing against the machine, even keeping running scores and records.

Then his Scrabble-playing friend sprung the trap. He asked if he enjoyed the game. The writer confessed that if it was a woman he would marry it. The Scrabble player said, "That machine is a computer. If you can operate that game, you can operate a computer." My writer friend was trapped.

He went to a computer store for a demonstration and selected a computer and word-processing software. He's not what I'd call a computer nut, but he now is a much more productive writer. He has since turned out a novel on his "new-fangled writing machine." And the computer not only saves him time and effort, but money: Before, he had to have everything retyped professionally.

What made the difference in him and in his writing productivity? Education. He learned what a computer is, how it works, and how simple it is to operate. That opened up a whole new way of writing for him.

Education also can make your professional life easier. Learning a little about your craft can increase the quality and quantity of your output. Your efficiency and efficacy increase in a geometric proportion to your knowledge. Let me give you a mathematical example.

If I asked you to give me the sum of all the numbers from 1 to 99 inclusive, it would probably take you considerable time, a goodly amount of writing, and, if you add like I do, quite a bit of checking, rechecking and correcting. And with all that, you might still come up with the wrong answer.

Suppose, though, I told you that I could show you a way to add all of those numbers quickly, accurately and without even using a pencil and paper. Would you believe me? Would it astound you?

Let's try it. You do it by recognizing certain sets of numbers within that list. There are pairs of numbers that add up to 100. The lowest number added to the highest number—that is, 1 added to 99 totals 100, doesn't it? The next pair—2 added to 98—does, too. Then 3 added to 97 totals 100, also. Correct? It should be obvious that this phenomenon continues right up to 49 added to 51.

So, you have forty-nine pairs of numbers, each totaling 100. The total of that would be 4,900, right?

That accounts for every number in the list except the number 50. You add that to the total and the final answer is 4,950.

It's logical. It's understandable. Anyone can do it, and you don't need a pencil and paper. And it's not a gimmick or an entertaining parlor trick. It's a solid mathematical principle that can be used by those who work with mathematics—computer programmers, accountants, actuaries and so on.

I would never have figured out this relationship of numbers on my own. I'd still be adding that column of ninety-nine numbers and cursing because each time I did, I'd come up with a different answer. I saw this relationship only when someone pointed it out to me. But that's education.

The same thing happened when I studied music. It will happen, too, when you study writing. The more you know about your profession, the more "gimmicks" you learn, the more you'll adapt them to your work, and the more they'll benefit you and your writing.

An experienced editor who hosted a one-hour seminar taught me something that immediately affected my own writing style: He taught me during his lecture how adjectives could be either useful or worthless.

Some adjectives, he explained, have a purpose. They're necessary. Before you gulp down your coffee in the morning, you want to know whether it's hot or scalding. Hot coffee is a pick-me-up; scalding coffee is dangerous. Those are useful adjectives because they definitely describe the noun.

"However," he said, "all mountains are majestic, all tears are salty." Many writers can't type the word "mountain" without the word "majestic" before it. It's not only clichéd, but it serves no descriptive purpose.

This taught me to think about adjectives as I wrote. I included the useful and discarded the worthless. I felt this made my writing more compact and consequently, more powerful. It also helped me to focus more on what I was trying to say and less on the flowery verbiage that I thought would be considered literate writing.

That's one idea I got from one lecture. We can glean more ideas from more extensive education. The more knowledge you get, the more you'll learn. There is knowledge hidden within the knowledge. The more you study about your craft, the more you'll come to realize that.

Education is always available to you regardless of your time constraints, money problems or geographic location. If you have the time and money, formal training is invaluable. Naturally, getting a B.A., an M.A. or a Ph.D. in English will help your writing. However, even taking a writing course or two at a local college is beneficial.

If you can't afford the time or the money for that, a weekend or one-day seminar can be useful.

There are even study courses that each writer can individualize to her own schedule. There are correspondence courses on various writing categories—nonfiction, short fiction, novels, children's writing and so on. With these you can learn from experienced professionals in your own home and at your own pace.

There are courses in which you work under the guidance of an established writer. For instance, you may begin work on a novel and have it analyzed and critiqued along the way by a published novelist.

The latest innovation is computer courses, in which you purchase software and follow its instructions. They may help you develop a plot for your novel, develop the characters, and even write your chapters. For those who enjoy working with their computers, this may be the perfect, painless education.

These are all formal study courses, whether you go to the classroom or bring the classroom into your own office. But there are informal ways to further your education, too. I've often told aspiring television writers that the best teacher they could hope for is sitting in the corner of their living room. Watch television, study the shows and learn from them. I heard a screenwriter tell students at her seminar that the best education for writing screenplays was a ticket to the theater. Watch movies. Learn how they're crafted.

Practically anything you want to learn about writing is contained in your local library. Read how-to books on the profession. Read biographies of other writers to learn their tricks and techniques. Read the work of other writers. If you want to write like Jackie Collins, read Jackie Collins. If you want to write like Stephen King, read Stephen King.

Everything you watch or read can be educational—the bad as well as the good. Learning what not to do can be as helpful as learning what *to* do.

Writer's Digest has a book club that offers the latest in writing technique books and other topics of interest to the profession. They send a bulletin each month that keeps subscribers informed of the latest books on writing.

Your education needn't be limited strictly to the writing profession. Study what you write about. The late Louis L'Amour's devotion to research gave his Westerns their authenticity. Tom Clancy's knowledge of weaponry and new developments in the military is so extensive that Pentagon personnel worry about where and how he gets this information.

The more you know about your subject, the better your manuscripts will be.

You can pick up a great deal of knowledge by subscribing to newsletters and joining associations. Newsletters usually have instructional and educational articles and exercises. So do many association periodicals. The associations, too, often offer discussion groups, lectures, seminars and workshops for writers.

Another helpful educational device is the advice of a qualified friend. I know many successful writers who have effective reciprocal arrangements. For example, one may ask the other for help in developing the plot. These writers submit outlines to one another, receiving back extensive notes and constructive criticism. They exchange manuscripts for comments. In effect, they educate one another, periodically flip-flopping the roles of writer and mentor.

Develop your education any way you can. That knowledge may just be the boost your career needs to get it moving faster.

CHAPTER 13

KEEP IMPROVING

We just devoted an entire chapter to education. Now for the bad news: Learning is only half the battle. Whatever information you acquire must be converted to a workable skill. It must become practical.

If you needed some sort of surgery, who would you opt to perform it? The young medical school graduate — the information is fresh in her mind — or the veteran surgeon who has successfully performed this operation hundreds of times?

Information is only a plan. Your architects may design a beautiful mansion, the house of your dreams. However, you can't live in a blueprint. You can't sleep in a drawing of a bedroom. You can't cook in a paper-and-ink kitchen. The plan must be converted to reality. Construction workers must level the land and pour the foundation. Carpenters must saw wood and nail it together. Plasterers must finish the walls, and decorators must paint and paper and fill the place with furniture. Then it's a home.

Writers, too, must act on any knowledge they acquire. If you learn something about writing, try it. Run it through your typewriter. If it works, practice and perfect it. Then it becomes another skill in your writing arsenal.

All of us have strengths and weaknesses, and that includes bestselling authors as well as struggling novices. Everyone can get a little better. For the writer who commands a seven-figure advance, the improvement may be icing on an already-successful cake; for the rest of us, improvement may be essential to moving up to the next plateau, to more success.

What are the steps to growing in writing skills? The first step is knowledge. Learn the craft of writing, the techniques required. Learn the business of writing—how the system works, how to market your product and so on. Learn the various avenues open to you as a writer. Should you write for magazines, or be the author of a book? Can you write for television or the movies? What about writing speeches for executives or presentations for corporations? Are there markets out there that you never dreamed of?

Knowledge is your blueprint. Now how do you build the house?

ANALYZE YOUR "GAME"

John Wooden of UCLA was probably the most successful coach in college basketball history. His teams won ten out of twelve NCAA championships from 1964 to 1975, including seven in a row. Today it's unusual for any team to repeat as national champs. Wooden accomplished this extraordinary coaching feat with diverse personnel. His first championship team starred small, quick, good ball-handling backcourt men.

Then for three years he built his teams around one of the most dominant centers in the history of college basketball, Lew Alcindor (who later changed his name to Kareem Abdul-Jabbar).

When Alcindor graduated, the UCLA team featured strong forwards. After that, Wooden coached Bill Walton, another center who was everybody's All-American.

Each team was different. They had different players who required different strategies. Yet, under John Wooden's tutelage, they maintained their twelve-year dominance over the NCAA.

How? Wooden analyzed his teams. Position by position, he recognized his players' abilities. With that information he organized a new plan of attack, one that capitalized on their strengths and minimized their faults. When you have a Lew Alcindor or a Bill Walton at center, you build your strategies around their skills. When you have a weaker player there, you build your strategies around other players.

Coach Wooden had successful years with Alcindor and Walton, but he had just as much success with lesser talents in the center position. The key to his success was his thorough and honest evaluation of each player's and each position's potential.

Suppose that Wooden had ignored this step. Suppose he said to himself, "I had a successful season last year with this strategy; therefore I'm going to use it again this year." His season would have been less successful, if not disastrous.

Sometimes our writing stalls because we don't effectively analyze our potential. We're not taking a hard enough look at our strengths and weaknesses. We're not building a program that capitalizes on our strong points and minimizes our flaws.

How do we do this? First, with honest, ego-free self-evaluation. Take a good, hard look at your writing. Are your plots intriguing and believable? Are your characters credible and interesting? Is your vocabulary crisp? Is your writing clear and concise? Does it convey what you want it to convey? Can you make the reader see, hear and feel what you want the reader to see, hear and feel? Where your writing is weak, be your own harshest critic. Where your writing is good, be your own biggest promoter.

Second, cold-bloodedly compare your efforts to top-quality writing. After you've written an essay, a magazine article, or a piece of fiction, put it side by side with one that you respect. How does it compare? Does it measure up to that piece of writing? If so, why? If not, why not? A truthful comparison will tell you much about what your writing needs and where your efforts on improvement should be focused.

Is this a harsh test? To compare one's writing with the writing of the absolute best? Not really. If you want to improve your writing and be numbered among the best writers in the world, you must measure up to them sooner or later.

FIND EXERCISES TO HELP YOU IMPROVE

Let's go back to John Wooden's coaching for a minute. Wooden, as good a coach as he was, wouldn't have captured the championship year after year just by analyzing his team's strengths and weaknesses and revising his tactics. He also had to improve his team.

In planning a strategy, a weakness can't just be identified and then left there. It must be improved, made strong enough at least to fit into the plan without being a major detriment.

One season, Wooden's ball handler—whose assignment on the floor was to control the movement of the ball—hadn't mastered use of his left hand. Wooden had him practice with his left hand only. He dribbled left-handed and even shot left-handed at all the team workouts. This player eventually became so proficient at using his off-hand that by the time he graduated, most people thought he was left-handed. That's practicing to eliminate a deficiency.

Likewise, advantages must be maximized. If you have a strategy that depends on accurate long-range shooting, your shooters had better practice daily so that they become dependable under game conditions.

Writers, too, regardless of their career plan, still should accentuate the positive and eliminate the negative. You can do this by finding or creating exercises—writing workouts, if you will—to strengthen various writing skills.

A book I've written, *Comedy Writing Workbook*, contains eighty-seven writing workouts designed to help develop various comedy-writing skills. These exercises can be done over and over again.

You may find exercises in other writing how-to books that will help you practice your writing techniques. However, you can also create your own. For instance, if you want to practice your descriptive skills, pick three places you go during any given day—the mall, the supermarket, your doctor's waiting room—and describe them effectively to your reader. Or randomly select three people you pass in the street, and describe them.

If you want to strengthen your vocabulary, select an essay from the editorial page and try to substitute different adjectives throughout the piece. Or use a new word each day, making it a permanent part of your working vocabulary.

To practice plotting, read only part of a short story, set it aside, and create your own ending for it.

To practice dialogue, set up an ordinary circumstance and try to write dialogue for it—dialogue that's interesting and tells a story. For instance, write dialogue for a father trying to convince his son after a Little League loss that winning isn't everything. Or write about a guy driving his girlfriend home from the airport with the dialogue revealing that the romance is over.

Going back to our sports analogy, a good coach decides what he wants his team and individual players to work on, then he devises drills to help them improve. The drills might isolate one particular skill, but they work on that skill until it becomes second nature to the athlete.

That's one way that you can improve your overall writing performance: by isolating and perfecting various writing techniques.

SET ASIDE TIME FOR IMPROVEMENT

Time can be the catch. There are only twenty-four hours in a day, and you have both your contracted work to deliver and your spec work that you want to get done. You need time to spend with your family and time for rest and recuperation. There simply is no time for practice.

Well, the simple answer is: There has to be. If you're not where you want to be now, you have to do something to get there. Unless you're totally depending on luck, you must make the effort to improve. You must make it happen. If you don't believe that, go back and read chapter one.

You must find the time to devote to refining your writing techniques. Here are a few tricks that might help.

Add to Your Working Time

If you begin your writing at 8:00 A.M., resolve to begin at 7:30. That will leave you an extra half hour of office time for writing improvement. Or, of course, you can add on to the end of your day. If you normally quit at 5:00 P.M., stay and do exercises until 5:30. You might even devote your break time to your writing drills. Ten minutes in the morning, ten at lunch, and ten in the afternoon.

You still have the same number of productive hours at your desk, but you also allow time for practice.

Combine Your Practice With Your Working Time

This may take some planning and creativity, but that's what writers are good at. Find some ways of coordinating your self-improvement into your productive desk time. For instance, arrange your exercises to apply to your required work. Instead of randomly selecting an exercise, choose one that can become a part of whatever "official" writing you do. If you're improving your vocabulary, why shouldn't those new words be used in whatever you're writing for sale? If you have to turn to your thesaurus anyway, why not learn a new word on the same page?

Once I took a home-study course in writing humor. Before I enrolled in the course, I made an arrangement with a local comic that he would have first-look rights at any and all comedy I generated as part of my homework assignments. He used the material, I got paid for it (which paid for the course and then some), and I improved my writing skills all at the same time.

Be inventive. You'll find ways that your daily writing can benefit your self-improvement, and your self-improvement can in turn benefit your daily writing.

Combine Your Practice With Your Relaxation or Recreation

Parlor games can be educational, and educational exercises can become parlor games. I watch "Jeopardy" religiously and somehow some of that knowledge those contestants exhibit rubs off on me. Not much, admittedly, but some.

I always do the "Word Power" section of *Reader's Digest*. It's a great way to learn more vocabulary words and more about them. Crossword puzzles, especially the tougher ones, do wonders for a person's vocabulary.

Even playing Scrabble has helped improve my knowledge of words.

Many of the exercises I've devised for comedy writers have become gamelike. People I've worked with have used them that way. Some writing friends of mine came up with a weekly game of comedy writing. We made a list of statements and then devised comic questions that they would be the answer to. For example, one statement was, "A hole in one." One of the questions a writer posed was, "What did Frank Ford leave when he met the James Brothers?" Each week one writer created a game, the rest of us played it, and on Friday we'd compare, and laugh at, our results.

With a little thought, you could devise writing exercises that are not only fun, but also educational.

Reevaluate and Rearrange Your Time Budget

Door-to-door encyclopedia and insurance salespeople used to use devices like these to sell their product: "And you can have this for no more than you spend now on your morning newspaper." "If you just eliminate one long-distance phone call each day, you could have this beautiful set of encyclopedias sitting in the corner of your living room." If you really wanted the encyclopedias or the insurance, this logic worked. If you didn't, you'd rather buy the newspaper or make the phone call.

You can trade time, though. It's there for your use if you just reconsider your priorities. You might exchange a half hour of sleep for improved writing skills. You might watch only the second half of a football game on television and devote the first half to your writing drills.

Time is available in your schedule. You just have to find it.

Use "Unusable" Time

All of us have an abundance of hidden time in our daily schedules, time that we think can't be used effectively. Then again, sometimes it can be. I suppose the classic example of that was "sleep learning," which was a fad a few years ago. Did it work? I don't know, but it was an attempt to use time efficiently.

Today, people who commute have learned to play self-help and educational tapes in their car. It's an effective way of acquiring knowledge while trying to control one's temper on the freeways.

I had a friend who learned to be fluent in a second language by listening to tapes when he went for his forty-five minute walk each morning.

I wrote my first book by using "unusable" commuting time. I dictated notes on a voice-activated tape recorder as I drove to work. I transcribed the notes and on weekends converted those notes into chapters.

Another time, I did a daily newspaper humor column by writing out a quick series of twelve to fifteen observations on a given current topic while I shaved in the morning.

Each of us has times that we can make more productive. You don't have to be obsessive and convert each nonproductive minute to an educational challenge. We all need time to smell the roses. But there probably are many times when you can smell the roses and write about them, too.

CHAPTER 14

LEARN TO LISTEN — AND TO HEAR

Once I dutifully walked a picket line when the Writers Guild of America was on strike. It's an unpleasant task, but one that for a while seemed to be part of every television writer's job description. While I was escorting my placard back and forth in front of a studio, a young man approached. He wanted to talk about television writing with some professional — although momentarily unemployed — television writers.

This young man was a student in one of the Writers Guild's free classes for the underprivileged. He showed us a treatment for a teleplay that he was particularly proud of. And he had good reason to be proud. His teacher had complimented the work highly and felt it had potential for a sale. The instructor, though, felt it needed more work and told this young writer to rework a few minor points and rewrite the treatment.

I said, "That's great. When do you expect to finish the rewrite?"

He said, "Oh, I'm not going to rewrite it. If my teacher wants me to do that, he's got to come up with some money first."

This lad refused to hear what his teacher had to say — and she was telling him good news. This instructor was an experienced professional writer, and probably one who was in a position, after the strike, to either buy this particular teleplay or hire this writer. But the young man didn't listen.

Some listen selectively. A young acting student had considerable beauty and charm but less acting ability. Her instructor was a perceptive veteran without a lot of tact. He spoke to her about her future: "You're a charming young lady. You have the beauty and the innocence of a young Bette Davis, but you have much to learn about acting. Your performances are superficial; you bring no passion to any of your roles. Good acting is reacting, and you have no perception of that. You perform in a vacuum. You take nothing from your fellow actors and you give nothing to them. Your interpretations are flat, lifeless and dull. I have taught many performers and have a keen eye for talent. That's been proven many times over the years. I honestly feel that you're wasting your time and energy pursuing a career that you're not suited for. I regret this harsh evaluation, but my reputation is based on honesty, and I would do you a disservice if I were less than honest with you."

When the student left this conversation a friend asked, "What did he say?"

The girl replied, "He said I was prettier than Bette Davis."

This girl listened, but heard only what she wanted to hear.

In the preceding chapter I recommended that you honestly evaluate your own writing and compare it to the work of proven professionals. Now I suggest that you welcome the judgment of others—good or bad—and consider their opinion when appraising your work.

Those "others" can be editors, producers, publishers, other writers, or simply friends and acquaintances. If they have an opinion of your product, consider it.

Notice, though, I said "consider." You needn't heed their advice.

But then again, why should a professional, knowledgeable writer consider the thoughts of others? One of the blessings of the writing life is that it's private. The author works alone, communing with the reader through the keyboard. It's completely entre nous. The thoughts of others are unnecessary, intrusive, unwelcome. Why should we allow them a voice?

Because it can be relatively harmless if you want it to be. If you get suggestions that you know are worthless, dismiss them immediately. They don't affect your writing. No harm done.

When I worked on "The Carol Burnett Show," one of our writers called his grandmother after the premiere show aired. It was the first time his name was listed on the credits of a national show and he wanted to share his joy with Grandma. He asked her, "What did you think of the show?" She gave a candid critique. She said, "It had too much blue in it."

None of the writing staff considered that admonition when assembling the next script.

Listen and decide for yourself.

Sometimes, outside advice can bring a different perspective. Because those "others" are not as close to the work as you are, they can often see it more clearly.

Also, others see only what is on the paper. The author isn't always that objective. Many times writers read their perception of what they *wanted* to put on paper. Writers know the characters and the story intimately. They have written background profiles on the principals and a detailed, chapter-by-chapter outline. Often they'll assume the readers know as much. They don't; they know only what's on the page. That distinction can make the readers' input invaluable.

Others, too, can evaluate a piece of work free from wishful thinking. Often the author can't. Authors want their work to be excellent, so they wish excellence into it—often where it doesn't exist. They want it to be good so badly that, in their eyes, it becomes good.

Once I got a page of jokes faxed to me with a plea from the writer to call him back that evening. When I did, he said, "I've written this material and am about to send it to (and he named a television comic). I just want your input because I totally respect your writing and I believe whatever you say about one-line writing. I'm getting rather desperate because I feel my writing is good, but I just can't get through and make that first sale. I think this is my best work, but I'll do whatever you say to make it better. Then I'll send it out and hopefully make a sale."

So I quickly read the seven or eight lines that he had faxed to me and I began. I said, "The first line, to me, is a little flat. It's a funny idea, but it needs more of a comedic twist."

He immediately jumped in, angrily, and said, "I worked on that line for two hours today and that's the absolute best I can do. That's the best *anybody* can do. That's a very funny line and I don't think it can be improved at all."

He hung up.

I didn't mind because it saved me the trouble of reviewing the rest of the lines. It made me wonder, though, about the logic of the call. Why ask for ways to improve lines that are unimprovable? It also made me wonder whether this writer really wanted my suggestions, or whether he just wanted my assurances that these were the greatest comedy lines ever penned and whoever didn't buy them was a fool to be pitied.

Another possibility — one that I have to swallow my pride to admit — is that my advice could have been completely wrong, totally worthless. Nevertheless, the author should have listened and filtered out the good advice, if any, from the useless.

This prompts a critical question: How do we decide which advice to heed? Here are a few rules of thumb that should help.

HEED EXPERIENCED PEOPLE

"Experienced people" doesn't necessarily mean the big shot with the huge desk and his name on the front of the building. Sometimes the executives and entrepreneurs know little about the nuts and bolts of the business. If your car stalls at every corner you probably wouldn't take it to Lee Iacocca for a tune-up. No, you'd take it to the mechanic you trust at your local repair shop.

Howard Cosell used to prattle on about the mistakes players made on "Monday Night Football." But there was no way he could ever know as much about the game as his coannouncers, Don Meredith and Frank Gifford. They had been there. Gifford knew how easy it was to fumble the ball when a 275-pound defensive guard just buried his helmet in your solar plexus. Co-sell didn't. Meredith knew how easy it was to overthrow a wide open receiver when a six-foot-nine fire-breathing lineman was rushing at your face. Cosell didn't.

Fantasize that you're on a 737 flying from New York to Los Angeles and there's an emergency. Everyone on the plane, including the entire cockpit crew, has come down with some rare, incapacitating disease. You must land the plane. When you sit in the pilot's seat and don the headphones, who do you want to hear "talking you down" — an experienced 737 pilot or your best friend from college?

I would heed what Neil Simon has to say about writing plays. I would listen to what Judy Blume has to say about writing juvenile novels. I would pay close attention to Erma Bombeck's thoughts on writing humorous books and columns.

There are people who have done what you want to do. They've done it successfully and for a long time. They've probably also struggled through the same troubles and heartbreaks that you're now enduring. If you're fortunate enough to get some advice from someone like that, listen attentively.

HEED THE DECISION MAKERS

The problem with writing for a living is that you must sell what you write. And the trouble with selling what you write is that someone must buy it.

In any sale, there is always that ultimate decision maker who gives the final approval for the transfer of money. This is the person who eventually says, "Yes, I like that piece of work and I will write you a check." It's also the person who says, "No, I don't want to pay any money for that piece of work." This is a person to heed.

Even though executives and entrepreneurs don't always know the business, and the person who issues a check may not know the first thing about writing, that person does know what writing she will issue a check for. Since you're the person who wants the check, listen to the decision maker's thoughts.

Writing is both an art form and a business. This decision maker may not be able to make you artistically better, but she can help your sales potential. If your writing is capable but not earning you enough money, this may be the person you especially want advice from.

HEED REPETITIVE COMMENTS

I recently sent out a piece of fiction to several editors. Some were mildly interested, but none bought it. All of the rejection notices, except the obvious form letters, had the same negative comment about one aspect of the piece. It was the same problem that a few friends and relatives who read it mentioned. I had omitted a key piece of information from the novel because I thought it was implied. It wasn't. Everyone who read it felt cheated.

Now I ask you, and I want your candid response: Should I make that change in the manuscript?

Of course I should. I left this particular piece of information out of my manuscript for a reason—I thought, a valid reason. I was wrong. When *everyone* who read the piece was bothered by this omission, it became obvious that this was a writing flaw to be corrected.

If you hear recurring comments from various readers, pay close attention to them. There's obviously some substance to the criticism.

I once received an angry letter from a comedy-writing hopeful. He had asked my advice about breaking into television. I offered him what I felt was realistic counsel. I suggested that he continue to write spec scripts. When he felt some were good enough, he should send them to several producers, and then be patient and persevering.

His response complained that I was offering him the same pap that other television people were tossing to him: write, write, write; persevere, persevere, persevere. He said, "I'm hearing this so often I'm getting sick of it."

Ironic, isn't it, that this same advice was mentioned by every "expert" this person queried, yet he refused to hear it.

HEED ADVICE THAT YOUR GUT TELLS YOU IS RIGHT

Admittedly, this is kind of a catchall suggestion. All of us, though, with honest reflection, will admit that it is valid. There are times when we know we need improvement or change, but we refuse to accept it. We know our plots are shallow, but we hope the editor won't notice it. We know we haven't researched this article very diligently, but we hope that our superior writing will disguise that.

I remember when I wrote my first sketch for a variety show. I was primarily a gag writer and I was learning sketch structure by trial and error — kind of on-the-job training.

I handed the sketch to the producers, who read it and were unhappy with it. "This needs a lot of work," one said.

I said, "I've already worked very hard on it."

The other producer said, "Well, it's not good enough yet."

I said, "I think it's hilariously funny. Name one thing that's wrong with it."

He said, "Well, for one thing. . . . " Then he began flipping through pages, not speaking. Finally he stopped turning pages and continued his sentence, " . . . there are twelve pages here where the star of the show doesn't say anything."

It was embarrassing, but it was enlightening. It not only showed me what was wrong with this particular sketch, but it showed me what was lacking in my education. It told me something that I knew inside: that I had a lot to learn about structure.

I heeded the advice. From that point on I thought less about "funny" and more about the basic structure of the sketch.

Some advice will hit you in the gut like a mule kick. You'll know it was coming. You were practically waiting for it. You won't like it when you hear it, and you might rebel as I did when these producers recognized my shortcomings. But you'll know it applies.

This advice, you should heed.

Most of us must improve in some area to enjoy more success. So be attuned. Listen to the marketplace when it tells you how to improve. Listen to editors, publishers, producers, buyers, other writers, friends, relatives, even a few strangers. Then filter the useful suggestions from the worthless, the wheat from the chaff.

Make your writing that much better, and shift your career into high gear.

CHAPTER 15

TRY TEACHING

Teachers are smart. Too damned smart. That's probably why as youngsters we disliked our instructors so much: because they always outsmarted us.

Consider the story of the four California high schoolers who went surfing early in the morning before class started. They enjoyed riding the waves so much that they stayed too long and missed an important test.

On the drive back to school they concocted a story that they went to the beach early in the morning, got a flat on the freeway, and couldn't contact anyone. That's why they were so late. They felt that anyone who fought the Los Angeles freeways would not only believe but sympathize with this tale of misfortune.

At school they pleaded with their teacher for a make-up test after class. He agreed. He sat each one of them in a different corner of the room and gave them a one-question quiz. The question was, "Which tire was flat?"

Teachers are clever.

How did they get so clever? In large part, simply by standing in front of the classroom. They've seen and heard it all.

It's almost impossible to instruct without learning something. Each year I organize a weekend seminar primarily for aspiring television comedy writers. A few of my writing colleagues volunteer as faculty members. It's a considerable donation of time and effort. I asked one man, who is a perennial, why he was so generous, not only to me, but to these aspiring writers who attend. "Why do you do it year after year?" I asked.

He said, "Because I learn so damned much."

TEACHING HELPS YOU ORGANIZE YOUR THINKING

Many crafts, writing among them, are principally "seat of the pants" skills. They call more for instinct than textbook. Practitioners do it without much thought to what they're doing or how they're doing it.

A friend of mine once wanted to make an instructional film for tennis players. He had a well-known professional self-analyze his serving motion. The pro was to go through his serving procedure on camera and talk about each step as he progressed.

It began well enough. He took his place behind the baseline and began. "First you assume a comfortable stance. Your left foot, for right-handers of course, should be slightly behind the baseline and pointed at the support post for the net. Weight should be on your forward foot. The feet should be about shoulders' width apart." He went on, technically explaining the correct stance before serving.

Then he told the viewers that he bounced the ball a certain number of times to relax his muscles and establish a rhythm. He explained how he held the ball for the toss and how his racquet hand coordinated with his tossing hand.

He was stymied, though, once he got the ball in the air. This was the point where he unleashed all his power and coordination at the ball to produce an accurate and powerful serve. He hesitated. He couldn't find the words to describe his fierce swing through the ball. Finally, in frustration, he said, "And then you just hit the hell out of it."

This touring pro didn't really know what he did to generate a powerful serve. His body knew because his serve was consistent. He did the same thing each time he served, and he did it well. But he wasn't aware of it. At least, he wasn't aware of it enough to verbalize it.

There's nothing wrong with intuitive skill. It's probably preferable to textbook technique because it's less complicated. Good writers are usually like that. They *feel* their best writing more than they *learn* it.

Purely intuitive skill is great—until it stops working for you.

Then you have a problem. How do you fix it? What do you change? Since you really don't know what you were doing, you don't know what's wrong with what you're now doing.

It's like driving a car. So long as you put the key in the ignition and the car starts and the steering wheel works, you know enough about cars to get you from where you are to where you want to go. But if you know nothing about engines and your car sputters and stalls, you're helpless.

Teaching can help you analyze and categorize your intuitive knowledge and skills. You must be able to do that in order to explain them to others. You can't get away with, "Just hit the hell out of it." You must provide vital, usable information. The information is there. You just never had a need to structure it. As a teacher, you do.

This new awareness can be beneficial when something goes wrong, as we saw with the car example, and sometimes it can help you improve your skills. For instance, the tennis player might realize, through teaching, where his power is being generated on the serve. Knowing that, he might be able to take steps to generate even more power.

TEACHING CAN BE INSPIRING

Once I was laboring on the staff of a top-ten television show. I use the word "laboring" because this particular day that's exactly what this group of writers was doing. The show hadn't "worked" at rehearsals, and no one was happy with it. The producers weren't happy, the actors were dissatisfied with the script, and the writers were embarrassed by it, too.

We struggled to make it better, but we weren't succeeding. We worked through the evening and into the early morning hours with little success. Finally one veteran television writer turned to me and said, "I just want to know one thing: When did my career become a job?"

That statement was funny and true. Do anything long enough and the luster begins to wear off it. The writing life that we all idealized becomes drudgery when the deadline becomes too real. Once our fingers floated over the typewriter keys. Now the keys seem to push back when we try to coax words from them. That can be a dangerous time. The frustration can show up in our work. It can hurt the quality and quantity of our product.

Teaching can renew our vigor because we usually work with bright, enthusiastic young talents who haven't yet lost their fervor. They may not have all the skills they need, but they have the zeal. That can rub off on you.

I remember the day my high school physics instructor explained to the class why a perpetual-motion machine was physically impossible. We listened attentively and learned that the most brilliant minds throughout history concluded that no machine could run forever on its own power.

That evening, nearly every one of us was working on his version of a perpetual-motion machine. Our efforts were purposeless but passionate.

Being a teacher, you can give direction while the class feeds you renewed excitement and intensity. Often a writer's professional life needs that infusion.

TEACHING HELPS YOU APPRECIATE YOUR PROFESSION

This benefit is almost the opposite of the one we just discussed, yet the two can coexist. Many of your students will have little interest in writing to begin with, and even less eagerness once they learn that effort is required.

Earlier I mentioned the generous faculty that works at our annual comedy-writing seminar. One year a lecturer challenged the attendees to develop their skills through the year. He offered them a series of exercises that they could take home and use as a self-teaching tool.

The following year, one of the students approached this instructor and told him, "That exercise you gave us last year was the most creative I've ever heard at a writing seminar. It was useful, it was beneficial, and it was challenging." The teacher thanked him and asked, "How did you make out with it?" The student said, "Oh, I haven't gotten around to doing it yet, but it was a really great exercise."

That can be disheartening to an instructor, but it also can be stimulating. How? Well, it can give us an appreciation for our profession and a genuine regard for those who are willing to do the work and make the sacrifices to learn and excel in this "not as easy as it looks" profession.

We can see another reason to take pride in our craft. It takes skill. It takes effort. It takes a person who is willing to stick with it to become a selling writer, a journeyman writer, an excellent writer. As we see others fall by the wayside, we can be proud to be among those who continue the adventure.

TEACHING HELPS YOU APPRECIATE GOOD MATERIAL

As a teacher you'll see bad material. Lots of it. It should remind you to keep the quality of your own material high.

I recommend to all the aspiring television writers that I work with that they emphasize two things in their writing: Follow instructions and avoid mistakes.

New writers, especially, must work extra hard even to have their material read. Once you get a buyer reading your submissions, you want her to keep turning pages. She is generally looking for an excuse to close the cover on your manuscript and toss it into the "polite form letter" pile. Not writing what she asked for or making glaring amateurish errors will give her that excuse.

Those are beginners' mistakes. Experienced professionals, though, can also fall into predictable sloppiness. Our work can become uninspired. We can sometimes be tempted to get by either on our experience or our reputation. That kind of shoddy work can eventually hurt our careers.

Seeing students' poor writing often can remind us that we constantly must work on our own quality control. That alone can be a giant benefit for a working writer.

I emphasize with comedy writers I teach that they force themselves to perform some of their own material. Go to an open-mike night at a comedy club or volunteer to do a short roast at a party for a friend. Talk at a church social or perform in the company's amateur show. Do anything at all, but stand in front of an audience and perform the comedy that you write.

I recommend this primarily so that they will experience the pain of performing comedy that doesn't work. Once they feel a joke bombing, they won't cut corners on work they try to sell to a comedian. That lesson will improve the quality of their work for a long, long time.

That learning experience may be unique to the comedy writer, or at least to those writers who deal in the performing arts. However, any experience that can bring a writer closer to the audience is beneficial. A teaching experience can do that.

Of course, not all teaching is the "stand in front of the room and write on the blackboard" type. If you have the qualifications, the inclination, and the time to offer accredited classes at a college or university, that's fine. But it's not the only way to teach and reap the benefits of teaching.

Here are a few other ideas.

Adult Education and Extension Classes

Many universities offer these classes. Often they're not accredited and are designed more for hobbyists than degree-seeking students. In Los Angeles, UCLA offers an extensive writing curriculum. It has many courses on entertainment-oriented writing, such as screenwriting, television drama, situation-comedy writing, and even stand-up comedy.

Teaching these courses requires time, for both preparation and classroom hours. The schools that offer the classes generally look for hands-on instructors—those with practical experience as opposed to academic qualifications.

Specialized Classes

Some organizations are always interested in classes for their members. For instance, local AARP chapters might welcome a class on magazine writing for their senior citizens. Youth organizations might like to offer a course on creative writing to their youngsters. Local writing chapters might be interested in having you teach a class in your special field of writing.

You have a skill that is rare and valuable. People everywhere want to learn what you do and how you do it. Teaching might help a few of them, and it will definitely help your career.

Specialized Classes in Writing Clubs

You may already belong to a writing club. Offer to teach a class in one of the writing skills to your fellow members. This doesn't imply that you must be a better writer than your colleagues. It simply means that you're the one who has volunteered to research, categorize and explain this area of writing to the others. You'll learn with them as the class progresses. However, the teacher is generally forced to learn much more than the students.

Teach at a Seminar

One- and two-day seminars have become popular, especially for writers. They afford an opportunity to meet editors, agents and other writers; to learn; and to ask questions about the craft of writing. Being on the faculty of such seminars is even more educational and beneficial than attending as a participant. I've served on the faculty many times for *Reader's Digest* writing seminars around the country, and for many workshops run by universities. Because the attendees are people who are willing to invest in their writing careers, the questions they ask tend to be penetrating and incisive. They force you to learn more about your own writing.

Another fringe benefit of working at these seminars is that you meet and work with many highly successful industry people.

Become a Lecturer

"Lecturer" is a highfalutin word, but it just means talking to people about something that you know about and that they're interested in. It's practically an informal chat with a lot of listeners. It's fun, and it offers all the benefits of teaching.

I've lectured to national and regional Toastmasters, to the National Speakers Association, and to several corporations, including AT&T and IBM.

Another fringe benefit here, for the writer, is the exposure. The engagements can not only be entertaining and educational, but they can lead to writing assignments.

Write Articles or Books

Teaching doesn't have to be done from the front of the classroom or from a podium with a microphone strapped around your neck. You can teach from the privacy of your keyboard.

I asked one writing colleague if he would volunteer to give a lecture at one of my seminars. He said, "Gene, I owe you a favor. I will come over and mow your lawn any weekend you want or iron a few shirts for you. Just please don't ask me to stand up in front of a group of people. I'm physically unable to do that." The fear of public speaking, in a poll taken just a few short years ago, was listed ahead of the fear of death. Many people can't speak in public, which can preclude teaching.

But this man can, and has, written articles on writing for magazines. That's teaching, and it carries many of the benefits of standing there with a pointer in your hand.

Help a Friend With a Writing Project

Once a collaborator and I were working on a teleplay and we had a problem with the second act. We couldn't find anything to resolve our premise. We were delighted with the first act, but couldn't get started on the second.

After much anguish, we called in another friend for his advice. We explained our dilemma and then handed him the unfinished script. He quietly read it and then said, "You have no problem."

We said, "Oh yes, we do. We're not happy with any of the directions the second act is going in."

He said, "You have no problem. This story is done." He suggested that we had a complete story compressed into the first act. It had a beginning, a middle and an end. The second act weakened our story and was totally unnecessary.

He was right. The reason we were having so much trouble with the second act was that we knew intuitively that it was not the completion of this story, but the beginning of another story. Once our colleague pointed this out, we rewrote the script and sold it. It turned out to be a delightful episode.

The point here is that writers can teach one another. You can be the instructor for a friend's writing project now, and he can be the instructor for one of your projects later.

If you're qualified, try teaching. Teach beginners, teach youngsters, teach anyone who can learn from your experience and know-how. You might find that you're the one getting the most education.

Sometimes that education may be just what's needed to get your career moving.

CHAPTER 16

SET A WRITING QUOTA

My grandson recently played in a weekend basketball game. It's a learning league for youngsters under eight years old. The basketball can sometimes be chaotic, but the kids have fun and learn the game in the process.

This particular day, though, his team took the court for warm-up drills and, as usual, the players were enthusiastic. They went through the warm-up as if they were playing in Madison Square Garden for the national championship. They were bouncy and energetic and couldn't wait to get the game started.

Then the game started and the other team scored the first 16 points. My grandson's squad was less bouncy.

The other team scored the next 8 points. My grandson and his teammates were downright glum. They all decided that basketball wasn't as much fun now as it had been twenty minutes earlier. All of the players figured that there was no point in running up and down the court any longer, so they didn't. They just let the other team run and dribble and shoot and do whatever they wanted.

My grandson's team lost 43 to 4, although I must add with some family pride and as a means of assuaging the boy for publishing this story, that my grandchild had all four points.

Defeat and failure can be frustrating and depressing. They can make you want to give up. Losing 43 to 4 is about as close to giving up as a team can come.

We writers feel the same way when we get a rejection notice.

We feel that way when our career slows down. But we're not kids in a learning league. We're professionals. We can't quit running the court. We must keep writing.

That's what a quota does for writers: It keeps them writing. It doesn't guarantee that the output will be superb. It doesn't automatically make you want to feel like writing. It doesn't magically inspire you to brilliance. It simply gets you writing. It forces you to put it on paper.

Many of us fantasize about the day when we won't have to worry about failure and rejection. But that will always be fantasy, never reality. Everyone in every profession, regardless of success, faces disappointments.

One day Bob Hope called and asked me what I thought of a new young comedian he was considering as a guest on one of his specials. I said, "Well, he has some good material. Other days, he's just ordinary."

Mr. Hope was silent on the other end of the phone for a second or two, then he said, "Gene, that's all of us."

There are disappointments in the writing profession. There are editors who don't like our submissions, critics who don't like our product. There are publishers who demand something other than what we want to give them, and there are periods when we're not happy with what's rolling out of our typewriter. There are days when we wish we had more time, and other days when we wish we had more talent. There are times when we wish all the keys would fall off our typewriters.

Despite the setbacks, the heartaches, the complaints — real and imagined — and the unrealistic demands, we must keep writing. We must keep turning out product. We must keep running the floor despite the 43 to 4 trouncing we're enduring.

One way to accomplish this is to set a realistic yet challenging writing quota. In chapter one we agreed that this was your writing career. Now you decide how much work you will produce daily, weekly, monthly. You determine, mathematically, what you must get done or want to get done, and set that as your writing goal.

This quota ignores emotions; it's above them. It doesn't consider setbacks; it has no time for them. It doesn't change whether the writing muse favors you or shuns you. Your productivity is your concern, not the business of some mythical, illusory spirit.

Neither is this quota just the writing equivalent of a pep rally to cheer on the team. It's a practical business reality, with down-to-earth benefits for writers, especially those in a writing valley.

You don't go to the supermarket and load up with a week's groceries, stand in line at the check-out counter and pay your bill, only to have the bagger say, "You know something, I really don't feel like bagging your groceries right now. You know what I mean? I'm not inspired to load cans of peas and corn into a biodegradable bag. The bagging spirit isn't moving me at the moment. I can't fill bags unless I feel like filling bags. I wouldn't want to do less-than-perfect bagging. So why don't you come back, oh, say, about 3:00. I just might be inspired by then."

This kid would have shredded wheat poured over her. You want your groceries loaded now, and this kid will load them now. That's her job, and that's what she'll do whether she feels so moved or not.

That's a writer's job, too. Your duty is to write, and you must write both when the spirit moves you and when it doesn't. You'll never sign one contract from a magazine or book editor that includes a "when the spirit moves the author" clause. They want words on paper, and your job is to put those words on paper. That's it.

So make a deal with yourself—set a quota—to produce a certain amount of work. Here's what this contract will do for you.

IT DISTRACTS YOU FROM YOUR DISTRACTIONS

The writing profession can be aggravating because much of it is out of your hands. It's frustrating to mail out a proposal or a query and wait what seems like twenty-six to thirty years for a response. And for some reason, waiting and writing often feel incompatible. A writer can't do one while doing the other.

Rejection is disastrous. It's always unjustified and usually spiteful—at least in our minds. We feel a need for revenge, so we get it by vowing not to write today, tomorrow or ever again.

Other elements can destroy our writing energy, too. The price of stationery can upset us so much that we abandon the writing life, at least temporarily. Our favorite pen runs out of ink. Someone in the family has borrowed and not returned our stapler. Practically any aberration can jar us off the writing track.

However, a quota is unsympathetic. It's like a drill sergeant who doesn't want to hear you whining about your petty problems. The quota says, "You have work to get done regardless of this, that or the other thing." So you get it done.

IT FORCES THE SPIRIT TO MOVE YOU

Writing is seductive. You begin to do it, with or without ardor, and soon it compels you to continue—with passion.

As a young electrical draftsman I had to organize engineering knowledge into a computer program that would simplify both the engineering and the drafting procedures. To do this, I had to interview many of the engineers. They had the knowledge that I didn't have. I had to pick their brains and then categorize and organize that information into a usable computer program.

They resisted. They said what they knew had too many variables to ever be so programmed. They were offended that I would try to trivialize their knowledge and feed it into an unthinking machine.

My strategy was to agree with them. There was no way that their information could be programmed. "But," I said to them, "if it could be, how would you go about doing it?" Then they offered me all the data they had and even suggested ways that it could be grouped together and arranged to fit conveniently into a computer program.

First they told me the work was impossible; then they did it for me. They got so involved in the process that they "did the impossible."

That's what a quota can do for a writer. It gets you writing. Whether or not you feel like it, and whether your output is good, bad or indifferent, it gets you tapping the keys. Soon — like their involvement captivated those engineers — the writing will entice you into the writing mode. You'll begin to get more and better ideas. You'll feel more for the words you're putting on paper. Rather than just going through typing motions, you'll be writing.

And sometimes you'll even surprise yourself. You may fulfill your quota with little enthusiasm — just writing to get the pages filled, not at all thrilled with what you write — but when you come back to the work later, you'll see that it's not as bad as you thought. It might have been just your mood the day you wrote it that made you dislike your output. That's why the quota is helpful regardless of how you feel. As a professional writer, you usually write professionally. You write compactly, following most of the rules. Your production may not be as brilliant as you would like, but you'll generally find, too, that it's not as bad as you thought it was.

IT GIVES YOU A MANAGEABLE SCHEDULE

I have a friend who jogs religiously and keeps precise records of his mileage. He averages more than 200 miles a month. I tell him he puts more miles on his Reeboks than I put on the family car. He runs about 10 miles on the days that he runs. He logs a respectable 2,500 miles annually.

Consider the predicament he'd be in, though, if he didn't jog daily. If he let all of his jogging go until the end of the year. He'd have to get up on December 31 and jog from Philadelphia to Palm Springs, then fly home in time to get dressed for that evening's New Year's Eve party.

It sounds silly, but we writers have a tendency to do that. We sell ideas, sign contracts, and then postpone the execution until the last minute. We don't put words on paper until the deadline is breathing down our necks.

A reasonable quota can break our projects into neat, workable, bite-sized chunks. When the deadline threatens, we have a manageable amount to do. We don't have to lace up our shoes and run from Philadelphia to Palm Springs.

When you work on a preprogrammed schedule, you can work in a more relaxed fashion and dedicate more of your time to a quality product. When you write under the gun, the manuscript doesn't have to be good; it just has to get done.

Your quota should be challenging, but not unwieldy. My friend jogs 10 miles a day because he's fit enough to handle that distance. If he set a quota for himself of 35 miles a day, rather than be in good condition, he'd be in a hospital. If he set a daily distance of 1 mile (which would be more my speed), it would hardly be worth his while to slip on his sweat socks.

Your quota must reflect your writing speed and conditioning, too. Too much or too little defeats its purpose.

For myself, I assign the number of pages that I can expect to complete working at a reasonable rate and allowing for a certain number of interruptions. If I complete that quota early in the day, I will probably continue working. That allows me to be nice to myself tomorrow, or the next day, or the end of the week. But I always force myself to complete the quota. I don't permit falling behind.

The quota and the way you control your system is a personal thing. It depends on your work speed and your work habits.

If your career is sluggish, though, it can be just the regimentation you need to push you into the next gear.

CHAPTER 17

EXPAND THE SCOPE OF YOUR WRITING

I kid about the beginning of my writing career. When people ask (and many times when they don't), I tell them that I got into writing for two reasons. First, I'm good at it. Second, I'm not very good at anything else at all.

That's a joke, and like most humor there's considerable truth in it. I did begin my writing career because I wasn't very good at something else. I was studying electrical engineering at the time and doing fairly well at it. I was an "A" student through high school and kept my grades up in college despite being a less-than-industrious student.

Then along came calculus. I understood the philosophy of calculus but could never master the details, the formula that would produce the answer. I knew what I should do and why, but I just could never learn how. I had been thinking for some time about pursuing writing, but the trouble I had with calculus convinced me to give the craft a try. I never went back to electrical engineering.

I remember well the beginning of the end—my first day in Calculus I. The teacher spent that first session lecturing us on the basic idea behind calculus. He knew it was a new form of mathematics to most of us. (In those days, they didn't attempt to teach it in high school.)

At the front of the classroom was a large blackboard that was four panels long. The teacher drew on it a small box, approximately 1 inch square, and said, "This box represents the mathematics you've studied until now." It was dramatic, but depressing. All of the times tables that I memorized in my early grade-school days, all of the algebra that I agonized over, all of the trigonometry and geometry that I mastered were all in that tiny box this teacher had drawn.

That was his point. "This box," he said, "represents your present knowledge of mathematics. In it are the basic rules and formulas that have to do with numbers, geometric forms and the like." He kept pointing at the box as he spoke. Suddenly, his arm swept to the large area outside of the tiny square. He said, "However, there is a whole world of mathematics outside of this box. This is what you're going to begin to study with this course."

He warned us that we would have to think for ourselves, invent new concepts, and explore questions with no defined answers. He challenged us to be patient with ourselves and with the course, to be open-minded and receptive.

Then he gave a lengthy lecture on the concepts that calculus would embrace. The lecture was overwhelming to most of us. One student in the back of the class raised his hand for a question.

The teacher pointed to him and said, "Yes?"

The student said, "Teacher, could you put us back in the box so we can rest for a couple of minutes?"

No matter what sort of writing you do, no matter how long you've been doing it, and no matter how successful you are at it, you're still in that box. You have an infinite universe of writing yet to explore. Every once in a while, climb out of the box.

MAKE YOUR WRITING GRANDER

I began my career with just about the smallest-sized writing imaginable: one-liners. The "pieces" that I worked on rarely went beyond two sentences. The first sentence would be the setup, the second would be the punch line. That would be the end of that comedic thought. Dismiss it, and move on to the next.

I clung to this writing form like a cocker spaniel guarding his favorite chew toy. This was my forte, my strength. Besides, it was good writing. My attitude was, "Any writer who has to use more than two periods in his work is simply wasting both writing and reading time."

Clients prompted me to expand my writing. Comics would say, "Why not write a piece of material for me?" A piece of material would be a monologue, a string of one-liners with a premise and a continuity. "Okay," I thought, "If that's what they're buying, that's what I'll write."

Then television forced me to begin writing sketches. These had more form and substance than monologues. They had to have a good, solid premise and structure. They needed a beginning, a middle and an end. And rather than just a string of one-liners, they required dialogue. Dialogue deals with exposition, emotions, character and of course, jokes.

But variety shows disappeared from television and I had to learn to write situation comedy to survive. Situation comedies demand even more structure than sketches. They must have a beginning, middle and end, but the middle must have more complications, more obstacles thrown in. So I learned to write situation comedies.

Following that, my agent suggested that I write a screenplay. Now they were pushing me beyond my limits. Screenplays are 120 pages long. That's a lot of writing for a guy who is used to two lines, tops. But I wrote screenplays.

Then a publisher suggested a book. Now they were getting ridiculous. Books were written by "real" writers, not guys who wrote one serious line followed by one funny line. I refused. I wasn't qualified. Then I wrote the book anyway.

Since that time, I've completed more than a dozen books. But I was lucky. Circumstances drove me into larger dimensions of writing. I was content with my two-sentence gems; the market wasn't. It demanded more, and forced me to do more.

You may be a writer who must drive yourself to larger dimensions of writing. And notice, each of the genres I graduated to was simply a larger-sized version of what I was already doing: jokes to monologues to sketches to situation comedies to screenplays. Even the first book was a collection of one-liners and humorous thoughts written into an essaylike form.

If you write short stories, perhaps it's time for a novel, or even a collection of short stories published in book form. If you write nonfiction articles, maybe one of your topics will support a book-length manuscript.

Whatever kind of writing you do, it can grow. Look at the work of other people who are doing the kind of writing you would enjoy. If they can grow into the larger form, so can you.

MAKE YOUR WRITING LOFTIER

I used to enter talent shows when I was a kid. All of us contestants knew we were dead meat as soon as one of the kids sang opera. The performer didn't have to be particularly talented; the classical touch alone would win the contest. No judge wanted to be the one who voted against operatic singing. Any youngster who sang "La Donne Mobile" had to be better than a kid who did an Al Jolson impression of "Swanee." Some music just seems to be loftier than others.

In many ways, this is true. George Gershwin was a piano player and writer of popular songs (songs being loftier than "ditties"). He was a good piano player, but he expanded his music to orchestral pieces like "Rhapsody in Blue," "An American in Paris," and "Piano Concerto in F." He wrote an American folk opera, *Porgy and Bess*, and wrote the music for *Of Thee I Sing*, the first Broadway musical to win a Pulitzer Prize. He expanded his musical output from songs to concertos to operas and musicals.

Some writing, like some music, appears loftier than others. I kidded a few paragraphs back about books being written by "real" writers. However, that concept applies. When my first book came out, my colleagues in television were delighted. One said, "A book, you can hold in your hands. What can you do with a television show except switch channels to see what else is on?"

I don't mean to label any type of writing as more substantial than another. Fiction is not loftier than nonfiction. Magazine writing is not more sophisticated than newspaper journalism. Adult prose is not more exalted than writing for youngsters. Poetry is not more artistic than prose. Each form of writing is unique.

However, in your own field and in your own mind, you may consider some areas loftier. If you believe this, expand your writing to at least give these other forms a try.

EXPAND INTO MORE INVENTIVE WRITING

Houdini was a masterful magician, an innovator in the field. Once, a competing magician began doing the same trick that Houdini was doing. So Houdini exposed him. He called press conferences and told the newspapers, and consequently the public, how this "fraud" was doing his trick. The "fraud" was exposed, while Houdini kept performing the trick. How? Houdini invented a new and better way of doing the trick. The other magician couldn't do the illusion because it was now exposed; Houdini now had an even better illusion.

That's innovation. That's expanding your craft into new, uncharted areas.

Writers can do the same.

At one time, the novel didn't exist. It's hard to believe as you browse through a bookstore and see the endless display of hardcover and paperback books of fiction that the art form only began in the eighteenth century. *Moll Flanders*, written by Daniel Defoe around 1722, is probably the earliest example of the novel written in English.

Just as the novel was invented, somebody someday will get tired of writing whatever we write now and will say, "I'm going to write something different." And that will be the invention of—something. We don't know what, but something.

Why not push yourself and your own writing to dare something new? What? I don't know. That's for each writer to discover for herself. In James Michener's latest novel, called *The Novel*, he creates a fictional writer who gains some notoriety by writing an extraordinarily offbeat book. In it, proper names appear arbitrarily and without definition; themes come and go; some pages are printed upside down, others sideways. Yet in Michener's story, this bizarre novel is published and becomes a sensation. That may be the way books are done in the next century. Who knows?

The point is that there are innovations out there, undiscovered. There are writing experiments to be tried. Many will fail; some will succeed.

Innovations shouldn't be introduced merely for shock value, but if a new device feels necessary to convey your ideas, try it. Expand your writing into pioneer territory.

Remember that box my teacher drew on the blackboard? It was comfortable in there, but it was monotonous. It was a land where everything had been discovered, where everything had been tried. The only way to explore and find new excitement was to get out of the box.

Give it a try occasionally and see if it doesn't help you shift your career into high gear.

CHAPTER 18

TRY A TOTALLY NEW ADVENTURE

I once heard a management expert give a seminar. He said during his presentation that the railroads were in the trouble they were in because railroad management made a serious error. "They made the mistake," he said, "of thinking that they were in the railroad business."

All of us in the audience thought that's the business they were in, too. The speaker explained, "They would have done much better if they remembered that they were in the *transportation* business."

Management, he explained, wanted to continue doing business the way the railroads had always done business. Many of those practices, though, were begun when the railroad was the major transportation force in the United States. Railroads and transportation were practically interchangeable.

Times changed. Airplanes moved cargo. Trucks became faster, and roads got better. Cheaper, faster, more appealing ways to ship materials became available. But the railroads refused to compete. They insisted on doing things the way they were always done.

That same inertia—doing today and tomorrow what we did yesterday—can affect our writing careers. We do what we do because we've always done it. Even when our careers stall, we continue doing what we always did. It's tried; it's true; it's traditional.

Why not toss a little adventure into the mix? Why not get radical? Why not get downright daring?

Ted Williams was a great baseball player, a Hall-of-Famer with the Boston Red Sox. He had a .344 lifetime batting average (which is eighth all time) and hit 521 home runs (also eighth all time). He was the last player to bat over .400 for a season. That was in 1941.

Williams was a tall, lanky, powerful hitter who pulled the ball hard to right field. That was the smart strategy for him. He hit hard when he pulled the ball, so many of his hits landed safely — often in the seats for home runs. He hit best when he pulled the ball to right.

So one manager created the "Ted Williams Shift." He put all of his players on the right side of the field. He was determined that with that many players over there, Williams would never get a hit to land safely. The shift didn't last too long, though. Ted Williams simply poked the ball to left field. There was no one over there to field it.

Williams decided, "If I can't go to right field, I'll go to left." He did something different.

If you and I can't get our career moving in the direction we've been headed, why not try a different direction?

Many of us fear change. We've got a fairly good thing going, so we don't want to jeopardize it. Change is a gamble; it's the unknown.

I remember when I finally got my first job in television. I had been working for an industrial firm. I was low on the corporate totem pole and was drawing a modest salary. My first writing contract for thirteen weeks was for about three times my then-annual salary, and it had much more growth potential. I was thrilled. When I told my mom, the first thing she said was, "Are you going to give up all that security?"

Security, to her, meant not changing the status quo. Don't take a risk, don't take a gamble, don't screw up what you've got. You may not have much, but at least you've got it.

The irony is that we can't avoid change. If we don't opt for it, it opts for us. That plant where I enjoyed my "security" employed 4,000 workers at that time. Today it employs fewer than 1,000. The factory used to occupy three city blocks. Today it is one small office building; the other three blocks have been converted to a public park. If I had remained there in an effort to avoid change, I would have been swept away in the changes that eventually occurred.

None of these suggestions imply that you should abandon your career and adopt a new one. But if your writing has slowed or stalled, some new and different adventures may rejuvenate it. If you're a nonfiction writer, try a novel or a short story. If you write serious political essays, give humor a go. If you write romances, try children's books. If you write poetry, try prose. Write a screenplay, a teleplay, even try selling a few jokes to a comic you like.

At first, these can be simple diversions, excursions into a new world. Families who go on weekend camping trips aren't necessarily announcing that they want to sell their comfortable ranch house and live the rest of their lives in a tent. It's just for the weekend.

Such tangential adventures offer the writer numerous benefits.

THEY CAN OPEN NEW AVENUES AND NEW OPPORTUNITIES

When I was a kid I hated lima beans. My mother asked me why I wouldn't eat them. I said, "I don't like the taste of them."

Mom said, "Have you ever eaten lima beans?"

I said, "No."

She said, "Then how do you know how they taste?"

I didn't; I just knew I didn't like them.

We must try things before we can pass judgment on them. Today I love lima beans.

A few years ago my brother was the president of a business organization. He organized its annual convention and invited me to speak there on "Humor in Management." He felt it was a different topic for the members; it would be both entertaining and educational. Besides, I could go to the convention, and he and I could spend some time together.

I was a comedy writer and I had worked in industry for thirteen years, but I didn't feel that I had much to offer as a lecturer. Nevertheless, I couldn't resist the chance to visit with my brother, all expenses paid. So I went, and I had a ball.

Oh, I enjoyed seeing my brother, but most of all I enjoyed being in front of an audience. This was heady stuff. No wonder entertainers got such a kick out of performing and hearing the laughter and applause. It was addictive.

I found out that many associations pay speakers a generous fee. So I investigated, did some marketing, wrote an entertaining little talk about the value of a sense of humor in our everyday lives, and today I am a "speaker."

Through this one adventure, I discovered a new, enjoyable, profitable world I never knew existed. I felt a little like Mark Twain, who said that once he discovered the lecture circuit he knew he'd never have to put in an honest day's work again.

Bold exploration can sometimes open opportunities, too. My friend and writing colleague, Martha Bolton, once wrote a letter to the editor satirizing a local problem. The editor published the letter and asked Martha to write a regular column for the paper. She offered to give it a try, though newspaper writing was neither her lifelong ambition nor her forte. The column, however, was funny and popular.

Some of her sample columns were her introduction to television writing. She was invited to send a few audition jokes to Bob Hope, he bought them, and today Martha is a staff writer for all of Hope's personal appearances and television specials.

ADVENTURES ALLOW US TO TEST OUR SKILLS

The old vaudeville joke goes:
    "Do you like Kipling?"
    "I don't know. I've never Kippled."

The only way to find out if you like Kipling, or if you're any good at it, is to "Kipple." Can you write novels, screenplays, children's books, humor, hard-hitting articles, poetry, song lyrics? You don't know unless you try. If you try a new writing form, you might discover you like it, are good at it, and are in demand.

My agent used to tell me that time off was like having a government grant. Television writing paid so well and worked on such frantic deadlines that writers welcomed the time off. Most of us took the money we earned and spent it on what we felt was a well-earned and much needed vacation. My agent urged me to use the time to write "spec" scripts. I rarely did.

One of my cowriters did. He had a successful and well-paying career in television, but during his hiatus, he wrote a screenplay. He received an Academy Award nomination for that film. He directed the next film he wrote. Today, Barry Levinson has an Oscar on his mantel and is one of the most highly respected directors in Hollywood.

ADVENTURES CAN BENEFIT OUR PRESENT WRITING

I once teamed with a writing partner who was a genuine world traveler. He spoke many languages and had lived in various countries. He had been a radio and television personality in Australia, a journalist in England, a hotelier in France. He could recommend the best restaurants in India. His anecdotes about people and places all over the world were fascinating. Just sitting in a Hollywood cafeteria or a Burbank coffee shop with this man was intriguing. Why? Because all of his far-flung adventures became part of his personality, his style, his flair.

That's how writing adventures can influence your technique—even if all of your adventures are abortive. You still learn from each adventure. Because you've explored other writing arenas, your everyday writing expands. You bring new points of view to your writing because you've explored the unknown.

So don't be afraid to take a chance, to wander off the pathways. You might find that there are interesting challenges out there. You might uncover opportunities you didn't know existed. You might discover skills you never knew you had. Better yet, the marketplace may discover skills it never knew you had.

To use another baseball analogy, a young player once tried something different. He was a promising pitcher — so good, in fact, that he had a 23-win season when he was only twenty-one years old. However, he liked to hit, too. Pitchers only play every four or five days and don't come to bat that often. So this youngster switched to the outfield, where he could get a few more swings at the ball. He tried something different.

It worked pretty well. You may have heard of him. His name was Babe Ruth.

The following chapter suggests some adventures for you to try with your writing.

CHAPTER 19

ANALYZE YOUR PAST WRITING FOR IDEAS

There's a story you might have heard about a not-too-bright factory worker who stuck his finger into the whirring blades of a fan to see if it was running or not. When his fingertip met the swirling metal it made an ungodly noise—*brzzzzzzzz*—and sprayed tiny bits of flesh and blood into the air. The injured worker yelped and a crowd gathered.

Then the supervisor pushed through the onlookers and said, "What happened here?"

The man said, "I just did this . . . " and stuck another finger into the fan to show the supervisor what happened. *Brzzzzzzzz.* The man yelped and said, "There. It did it again."

Dutch philosopher Baruch Spinoza said it less comedically: "If you want the present to be different from the past, study the past." Spinoza became a part of the past way back in 1677, but his advice has merit for today's writers.

The factory worker in the opening anecdote seems dumb because he didn't learn anything from his traumatic experience. He immediately repeated it. It does seem stupid, but many of us do the same thing. We either fail or refuse to learn from history.

Tennis teacher Vic Braden tells about a student who complained to him: "Vic, I've got eleven years of experience playing tennis, but I don't seem to be getting any better." Braden said, "No. You've got one year of experience eleven times."

Experience is a great teacher, but we must make an effort to be great students, too. Experience can't teach anything to someone who refuses to learn.

As a reasonably successful writer, you have a past, a portfolio of work. If you're like every other writer alive, your previous work consists of some good writing and some bad. There are lessons hidden in every page. Study your material. Reevaluate it. Find out what was good about it, what not so good. Learn what the editors liked about your writing and what they disliked. What kind of fire did you have in your soul when you wrote, and how can you recapture or rekindle it? How has your writing changed? How have you changed?

Following are suggestions to use in reviewing your earlier work, with an idea toward improving your present work and getting your career shifted into high gear.

RECAPTURE THE ENTHUSIASM

Here's another anecdote. This one's about two bulls grazing on a hillside overlooking a herd of cows. One bull is old, the other young. The young bull interrupts his grazing and says to the older one, "Hey Pops, what say we run down there and take care of a few of those cows?" The old bull finishes chewing on a clump of grass, eyes the younger bull, and says, "What say we *walk* down and take care of *all* of them."

Youth has exuberance; age tempers it with wisdom. Both are valuable, and the combination of the two is powerful.

As a television producer, I tried to assemble a staff of writers that merged old pros with promising young comedy writers. The youngsters wanted to do wild, zany, bizarre comedy; the old-timers preferred to stay with proven, time-tested techniques. They'd argue and butt heads, and the eventual compromise would be somewhat wacky but well written and workable.

Individually, the youngsters would have been so off-the-wall that their ideas wouldn't work on television. They were too bizarre, too strange, too much of a burden to put on the average viewer. And the old-timers would be worn down by the medium. They'd have written what was written before. They knew better than to rock the television boat. Consequently, their writing would have been predictable, rehashed, tired.

That's one of the negatives of experience: It can rob you of your exuberance. Among the things it teaches you is to remain traditional. Write what people are buying and write what people are used to reading. It's commercial and it's wise, but it sometimes lacks spark.

A journeyman writer is satisfied to write a book that is bought and published, and that sells a respectable number of copies. A first-time author always writes, in his own mind, a "best-seller."

At this phase of your career, you may need some of that spark. You probably found it in your earlier writing. Some of your previous writing may not have been technically as polished as your writing is today, but it may have had more zing to it. That's what you'd like to recapture and inject into your more mature writing style.

In reading some of your past material, find out what excited you then, what got the enthusiasm coursing through your veins. Replicate that today.

Let me give you an example. When I first began writing comedy material, I was freelancing, so no one dictated to me what to write about. I selected the topics. Naturally, I selected those subjects that interested me. I searched out areas that I felt I wanted to write about, that I thought were deserving of a comedy routine. And I wrote about those.

Today I write what I'm assigned to write. Clients call each morning and say, "Write about this, this and this." It's not always easy to get interested in these subjects, nor to find anything particularly funny about them. The jokes get written, but they're not always inspired.

Being aware of this, I devote a little of my workday to writing about things *I want to write about*. Even if I never sell one of them, they make my contractual writing better because they reawaken my enthusiasm for comedy.

If you can't write about what excites you, find some way of making the writing you must do exciting. I know some of the Bob Hope writers use this device when faced with a tedious assignment. One puts on a videotape of a good Hope monologue or dialogue with a guest. As he listens and enjoys, he notices that Bob Hope is a master of timing, a legendary comedian. He remembers that he's writing for the best, so he wants his material to be the best. He now approaches his assignment with more vitality.

I sometimes put myself on the stage in place of Hope. I picture myself reciting the one-liners or trading quips with some movie star, sports standout or well-known politician. When it's me on stage with these greats, I want the material to sparkle. Consequently, when I write it, I have more enthusiasm.

LEARN WHAT YOU DID BETTER THEN

You're a better writer than you were a few years, or even a few months, ago. So what can you learn by looking backward? Well, it's possible to get better and worse at the same time. I know it sounds like drawing a square circle, but improvement and deterioration can happen simultaneously. In fact, improvement can sometimes *promote* a lessening of certain skills. You can get so proficient in a certain skill that you become less dependent on other ones. As a consequence, those others atrophy.

For example, when I was a draftsman, I made blueprints for a living, so my printing had to be clear and legible. Now I'm a writer. I work at a typewriter or a word processor constantly. My typing speed has increased tremendously, but my handwriting is now completely unreadable. If I scratch out a joke on a piece of paper, I either have to transcribe it that same day or lose it.

You see the same phenomenon in most sports. In basketball, for example, the taller players stay near the basket. Someone throws them the ball and they turn around and stuff it into the basket. They never have to dribble, so they don't practice dribbling. The smaller players do that. As the big players get better and better at stuffing the ball into the basket, they get worse and worse as ball handlers.

It happens to writers, too. As we get better in one skill, we sometimes neglect another. Not because we're lazy or complacent; it's just that we don't need that skill as much anymore.

I knew some good gag writers who graduated to writing successful screenplays. They're now excellent screenwriters, but could they turn out several pages of one-liners on a moment's notice like they used to? Probably not.

You, too, have grown as a writer. You've improved certain skills. In the process, though, you've probably lessened a few. That's not bad, because the ones you've improved are probably more important than the ones you've neglected. A seven-foot basketball player should be around the basket, not dribbling the ball somewhere around midcourt.

Nevertheless, the more skills you can master, the better you'll be. Magic Johnson was listed in the program as six-foot-nine when he played for the Los Angeles Lakers. That's tall — even for a basketball player. Yet he could dribble, pass, shoot from outside, and also go inside to rebound and tangle with the "wide bodies" under the basket.

It pays to review your past work to see which skills you had that you've lost. A few might be valuable to you today, and they can be resurrected. It can make you a better writer.

NOTICE HOW YOU'VE IMPROVED

This is a morale booster more than a technique developer. It's encouragement more than education.

I work with many young comedy writers. They send me pages of jokes and ask for evaluation. Often, I'm tempted to write back with the traditional advice, "Stick with your day job."

Then I dig out some of my early comedic efforts. They're often not as good as the material I've just evaluated.

When I see how I've improved, I know that this other writer can improve, too.

You'll probably notice in reviewing your previous efforts that you've improved tremendously. You're a better writer today than you were then. By projection, that means you'll be an even better writer in the future than you are now.

It just might be that prod you need to keep on working, keep on trying and keep on marketing.

LOOK *INSIDE* YOUR WRITING FOR FRESH ADVENTURES

The arts are famous for pigeonholing. If you write romance novels, you're a romance-novel writer. If you write spy thrillers, you're a spy-thriller writer. Do you write juvenile novels? Then how can you ever hope to become an author of adult novels?

I worked with a writer who was once a successful musician. He played with several of the big bands during that era. When he tried to get a job as a studio musician, people said, "He's a big-band drummer, not a studio drummer."

He worked his way up the ladder step by step, but told me that at each step he was stymied by the narrow-mindedness of the buyers. Finally, he landed a job as a studio drummer. When he tried to go on the road again with some bands, they said, "He's a studio drummer, not a big-band drummer."

Same guy, same skills, but pigeonholed.

What's more dangerous, though, is when we pigeonhole ourselves. When we say, "This is the kind of writing I do; this is the kind of writing I'll always do." That's simply not true — or at least, it doesn't have to be true. There are clues in your writing that can direct you to thrilling new writing avenues.

If your dialogue crackles, maybe you should try some plays, screenplays or television scripts. Do you editorialize? Maybe you should write essays or do a newspaper column. Is there a lot of whimsy in your storytelling? You might be able to write some delightful children's books. If your writing has a lot of wit, you might try humor or comedy writing.

The possibilities are limitless; you must look for them in your own writing. You just might find your avenue to fresh adventures.

LOOK *OUTSIDE* YOUR WRITING FOR FRESH ADVENTURES

Your writing past is limited. You've written only so many pieces about so many things in so many different genres. Every writer's past is limited, regardless of success or diversification.

When you review your writing archives, you'll see all the places you haven't been, all the things you haven't done. That alone may inspire you to try something new.

In my own career, I've written for many television shows and show-business personalities. I have a collection of twenty-eight volumes of one-liners I've written for just one comedian. I've had more than a dozen books published. I've written countless episodes for television situation comedies.

But I don't have a novel published. That may be my next adventure.

Reading through your backlog of material may lead you to new writing terrain. In any case, it will get you thinking about your writing techniques and markets, and will help get your writing into high gear.

CHAPTER 20

FORCE NEW COLOR INTO YOUR WRITING

When I graduated from high school, I joined the family work force. Mom and Dad worked then, too, so we all had various chores to help around the house. My dad was the earliest to rise, so he put the coffee on and packed lunches for the rest of us.

The lunches were simple enough: a sandwich, a piece of fruit, and some cookies or a small pie or cake. One day Dad packed me a boiled ham sandwich and a coconut custard pie. For whatever reason, it hit the spot that day. It tasted delicious.

I told that to Dad when I got home and, boy, was he proud of himself. I never realized that such a small compliment could mean so much to a person.

However, the next day I had a boiled ham sandwich and a coconut custard pie. And the day after that, and the day after that, and all the days after that. Mom and my brother got different sandwiches and desserts each day. Not me. I got boiled ham and coconut custard pie.

I couldn't think of a diplomatic way to tell Dad that I wanted some variety. He was still too pumped up from the compliment I had paid him. It would break his heart now to know that his lunches were no longer "gourmet fare."

Even so, it tasted good for a while because I liked boiled ham and coconut custard pie. Quickly, though, it became disappointing. I'd open the bag and unwrap the wax paper hoping to find something else—Swiss cheese, roast beef, anything besides boiled ham and coconut custard pie. But it was always boiled ham and coconut custard pie.

It became difficult to chew, then impossible to swallow. I grew to hate the taste of boiled ham so much that for years I couldn't eat the stuff. And I began rejecting not only coconut custard pie, but any custard pie. I couldn't get it from the plate to my mouth.

I finally devised some story so that I had to get up earlier than Dad. I inherited the lunch-making chores and could make my own midday snack—although I always told Dad that mine were never as good as his had been.

What happened? The lunch meat and the baked goods were nutritious and I once found them delicious. Why didn't I after a while? Because they became cloying. The monotony of it altered my taste buds. I got sick and tired of boiled ham and coconut custard pie—just as you're getting sick and tired of hearing those words.

We all have a tendency to become predictable. When I drive over frequently traveled routes, I tend to change lanes in the same places on the freeways. And tennis opponents know before I do where my shots are going.

When you start or stop your car, you probably go through a series of automatic moves, moves you hardly know you're making. I drive a car with a foot-operated emergency brake pedal; my daughter has a hand-operated one. The few instances when I've driven her car, I've almost put my foot through the floor boards trying to set the emergency brake that isn't there.

We all become creatures of habit.

Our writing can become predictable, too. Not that it is necessarily as cloying as my repetitive ham sandwich and custard pie diet, but it can have a sameness to it.

My youngsters, when they were in junior high, became experts at spotting predictable patterns. I remember once watching an episode of "Barnaby Jones" with them. The story opened with Barnaby visiting a friend who owned a ranch. The friend was showing off a white stallion that was trained to rear up and kick its forelegs on command. My daughter said, "The horse is going to kick the gun out of somebody's hand." Sure enough, some forty-two minutes later, the stallion saved Barnaby and friends by disarming the "baddies."

Watching another mystery show—I don't remember which—my kids again predicted the denouement at the very opening. The characters were gathered on a seaside balcony to take photographs. There was a solitary sailboat in the background. My daughter said, "The killer is on that boat." He was.

Certainly, pipework must be set down in a mystery teleplay, but when it becomes this transparent, the format may be overused. It needs new devices, new color.

We should look at the same thing in our writing. My one-liners often have to be completed quickly. I have a tendency to lapse into one dominant style of joke. I write in a very literal style. The jokes are realistic. For instance, I might do a joke like, "If the government really wants to simplify our tax returns, why don't they just print the money with a return address on it?"

That's a usable joke—a good one, I think—but it's possible. The government could conceivably print money with a return address on it. That type of joke is fine, but it becomes monotonous quickly unless merged with some wacky, zany, downright impossible gags. For example, "It's easy to tell when it's tax time. The statue on top of the capitol building is wearing a stocking over its face."

In rereading my comedy monologues I sometimes notice that I have too many of one type of joke. The routine lacks variety, interest. It's too monolithic.

Often I fall into the same trap in writing prose. I overuse a certain sentence structure, or all of my sentences are of relatively the same length. Sometimes in my dialogue writing, I'll notice that all of my characters have the same speech patterns even though they're very different from each other. That's my fault as a writer.

I must force myself to search for wild, off-the-wall jokes for my monologue routines. I must deliberately vary my writing style to keep the sentences from becoming too staccato, too rhythmic. I must listen to my characters and write down what *they* would say rather than put *my* words in their mouths.

Too many of these habits can produce writing that is bland, that makes for dull reading. What it needs is a dash of spice.

How do you add a dash of excitement to your writing? First, like a good chef, you must be aware of the spices available to you. I'm not much of a cook and I notice when I watch a cooking show on television, I have to ask my wife what half of the ingredients are. I've never heard of many of the taste-ticklers the chefs add to their dishes. If I've never heard of them, I can hardly use them in a recipe I invent.

You can become aware of good writing devices or techniques as you read. There probably are as many of them as there are writers. As you become aware of literary devices and techniques, you'll absorb more and more variations that you'll want to incorporate into your writing. You'll notice how some authors use short sentences for fierce impact, while others use long, descriptive phrases to draw the reader along.

You'll become aware of the potency of verbs. You'll notice intriguing sentence structures. Sometimes you'll even see punctuation that fascinates you.

These are all spices that you can use in cooking up your literary recipes. Try them out. Season your own writing to taste.

Once I accompanied an aspiring self-taught artist when he sought employment with an advertising agency. He brought along some paintings. I thought the paintings were superb. They looked like what they were supposed to look like, and they were pleasant to look at.

The advertising executive, though, saw something else. He was polite and helpful, but he criticized the artist's work.

He said, "You come to the surface too soon."

Neither one of us knew what he meant, so he explained it.

He said, "You don't lay enough paint on your canvas. You paint a layer of blue sky, then a white cloud. You paint a field of grass with two shades of green: light and dark. Everything is flat. Your grass should have many tones in it—greens, yellows, browns, blues, whatever colors will make it interesting and bring it to life."

You may have to force yourself to study the masters a little more and bring more variety into your work. Add more layers of paint. More color. It may help bring your writing to life.

PART III

LOOK TO YOUR MARKETING

"The two most beautiful words in the English language are: 'Check enclosed.' "

DOROTHY PARKER

CHAPTER 21

BE PROFESSIONAL

Once I was writing a television variety show and my partner and I, together with the producers, cast the leads. We were looking for a comedy team to host the show.

We interviewed one team who had a hot comedy record that was getting considerable play on the radio and a lot of notice. They must have felt that our show was beneath their dignity. During the interview they were rude, arrogant and chastised us for even considering them.

They said, "Look, we do a specialized kind of comedy and we don't think you can write that." They certainly knew how to endear themselves to the writers. They went on: "Besides, we're above this kind of a show. Our record is hot and we're red hot. Frankly, we don't think you can afford us."

We were stunned and before we could compose ourselves for a rebuttal, they were out the door. We just stared at each other in shock.

Then the door opened and one of them came back into the room holding a parking stub out to the producer. "Oh, by the way," he said, "do you validate for parking?"

I honestly can't remember their names, but you probably wouldn't recognize them anyway because after their hot record cooled, so did they.

Writers, like performers, sell more than their product; they sell themselves. Performers, of course, must sell in person, but writers can market their wares through the mail or over the telephone. Many writers have worked with editors, publishers, agents and others for years without ever meeting them face to face.

Nevertheless, in all exchanges, whether it be over lunch, in an office, via the mail, or on the telephone, each of us should remember that we're dealing with professionals. Each of us should not only treat that other person as a professional, but act as a professional ourselves.

What is "professionalism"?

Once I heard a definition of "class" that intrigued me. Mortimer Levitt, founder of the Custom Shops, said that class wasn't arriving at a fancy ball in a Rolls Royce with a uniformed chauffeur opening the door for you. He explained that those things were the accoutrements of class. "Real class," he said, "is how you treat your chauffeur."

Professionalism is how you treat the people you deal with in your profession — publishers, editors, agents, other writers, secretaries, everybody. It's recognizing that writing is your profession and treating it as such. It's also realizing that these other people you deal with are professionals. They have a business life that has time and budget constraints. They have a job to do that is stressful and sometimes emotional. They must deal not only with you and your concerns, but others and their concerns. Professionalism is treating them all with dignity, respect, courtesy and consideration.

"Consideration" is the key word whenever you're in doubt about acting professionally. *Consider* the other person. What is her workday like? What problems does she have doing her job? What would make her life easier? Once you consider things from her point of view, you'll know how to treat her professionally.

Here are a few suggestions.

PRESENT YOUR MATERIAL PROPERLY

You want people to read your material. You want an agent to read it so he'll do anything to represent you. You want a publisher to read it so she'll send a book contract. You want an editor to read it so he'll publish this article and immediately ask for more. Therefore it seems to be common sense that you should submit in whatever form makes that reading as easy as possible.

How do you do that? Give it to them in whatever form they want. Some of the professional standards are universal:

Your submissions should be neatly typed—never hand-written—and readable. Today's technology offers many types of printers. All of them are acceptable, unless the printing is a burden to read. Dot matrix, of course, is usually the culprit; however, even that is acceptable if the density is high enough that the letters are easily readable and appear typewritten.

Computer technology, though, also makes other typefaces readily available. With today's software and advanced printers, you can print your manuscript so it looks like it was printed by an expert calligrapher. You can make it look like it was printed in Old English by medieval monks. You can make the printing heavy and bold as if it were done by a sign painter. All these type styles are gimmicky. They serve their purpose, but not in a manuscript. They should be avoided unless specifically requested by a client. Fancy type styles, like Script and Old English, are annoying when an editor is used to reading standard typewritten pages. Whatever computer system you use, be sure that it has a typeface, whether standard or proportional spacing, that resembles an old-fashioned typewritten page.

Most editors prefer standard typing—lowercase with capitals where appropriate, double-spaced and with generous margins. And most request that the manuscript pages be unattached—no stapling or binding. This is so the manuscript can be disassembled for easier reproduction or for distribution to several readers.

Each page, also, should be identified and contain a page number. If manuscripts are not bound, they're vulnerable. They can be dropped, blown around by a fan or an open window, picked up accidentally along with other papers, or thrown across the room by an irate editor. If they're identified and numbered, they're much easier to put back together again.

Manuscripts should be as free of errors and overwriting as possible. Computers are helpful here, because errors are easily found and corrected, and retyping is painless and fast. So any mistakes you discover should be corrected. A few penned-in corrections are allowable, so long as they don't make it a chore to read through the manuscript.

Usually, return postage is required. If you're in doubt, include it. Again, though, computer technology affects this tradition. With large manuscripts writers may include a self-addressed envelope with enough postage to cover just a reply rather than the entire manuscript. It's often cheaper to reprint the text than it is to pay for the return postage. In that case, it's acceptable to notify the editor that she may discard the manuscript and simply send a letter in the enclosed SASE.

Some people want the material the way they want it regardless of professional standards. For instance, I have one client who insists on the largest typeface possible and with everything written in capital letters. So that's how I submit it. Another client hates double-spacing, so I submit single-spaced.

How do you find out these specific requirements? Ask. Most publishers will publish a list of writers' guidelines that cover these specifics. You may obtain them before querying. Or if you make a sale, ask for them before preparing your manuscript.

In either case, treat all requests professionally; don't ignore some of them simply because your computer parameters are already set. Change your margins if you must, change your typeface. Give the clients what they want. It's professional. It's considerate. It's good business.

RESPECT OTHER PEOPLE'S VALUABLE TIME

I often receive letters from writers asking for advice, information, a critique of a writing sample or the like. Some of these letters are six pages long. They give details of family tragedies, troubles with intolerant teachers in grade school, problems on the job, with their children, with their wives, with their health. Without seeming too cold-blooded, I must say I don't care about these things—and neither do most editors, publishers and agents.

These details are irrelevant; they waste the writer's and the reader's time, and that's unprofessional.

Professionals care about the profession. They care about what you can put on paper, not how you put it there, why you put it there, or why you've been forced to put it there.

As a professional, there are times when you must impose on another professional's time. The editor must read your query letter; the publisher must read your proposal; the agent must talk to you on the phone. However, you should keep all communications crisp and businesslike. Assume that even if you have time to waste, the person at the other end of the communication doesn't.

Don't become a professional pest. Eliminate unnecessary meetings and telephone calls, and cut down unreasonably long letters. Find out what you need to know as quickly and as easily as you can, and then allow the other person to get back to work.

In ongoing relationships, find out how your associates prefer to work. Do they prefer letters, fax communication or telephone calls. I know most books advise against telephone calls, but I've had some editors tell me that with writers they know and work with, a call is less time-consuming for them. They pick up the telephone or take a message and call you when they have time, answer your question, and get back to work. There's no paperwork, no dictation, no proofreading of the letter, and no waiting for the mail to deliver the exchange.

When you work on the telephone, be efficient. If you have questions about expenses, do your figuring before placing the call and have a calculator nearby in case the person you call suggests some changes. If you have questions about the manuscript, have it in front of you with the page numbers marked and readily available. Be prepared, and save both of you time.

Of course, other editors may not like the intrusion of the telephone into their busy schedule. They're better equipped to deal through fax correspondence or mail.

Each exchange will be slightly different, so determine the best modus operandi by asking. That's being considerate; it's being professional.

PRESENT YOURSELF AS A PROFESSIONAL

Can you imagine going to the ball park and watching the Yankees take the field in their legendary pinstriped uniforms, only to see their opponents wearing blue jeans and T-shirts of assorted colors and markings? You wouldn't stay for the game. You'd ask for your money back. This is not big-league ball; this is not professional.

Professionals have an obligation to look like professionals. I remember once sitting in on a practice session of my college basketball team. They were ranked in the top ten at the time and were a major force in college basketball. At the end of practice, their coach told them they were all scheduled to attend some sort of meeting that evening. He warned them, "Wear a clean jockstrap and show up in a shirt and tie." The jockstrap reference was a joke, but he was serious about the shirt and tie. He wanted his team to look like a number-one team.

You should look like a professional writer, too. Have neat, dignified business cards and stationery printed. With astute shopping, stationery is not that much more expensive than plain paper. You can design your own, have it professionally designed, or buy from a printing shop that has prepared standards that you can select from. Whichever you do, keep it simple and dignified.

I've seen some letterheads that list a whole string of accomplishments: "John Doe—professional writer, speaker, lecturer, teacher, television performer, part-time juggler, kitchen appliance demonstrator, former vice-president of the United States." Well, it doesn't get that silly, but almost. Give the vital information—name, address, telephone number—and maybe a neat design or simple logo. Let the text of your letter do the rest.

When I first began writing comedy I had an artist prepare a pen-and-ink cartoon of a jester. It was smaller than a dime. I put that on all my stationery as my logo. It said "comedy," but in a muted tone.

Later I discovered that my first two major clients—the ones who paved the way for my entrance into television writing and a professional career—said that the logo was instrumental in their hiring me.

One said whenever she saw the envelope with the little jester in the corner, she would open it first and read the material. The other said when he was rushed for new material, he'd leaf through his collection of papers and pull out the ones that had the jester in the upper left-hand corner.

The logo was dignified, professional and apparently unique enough to get noticed. More important, it got the material noticed and read.

Not all of a writer's work is done through the mail, over the fax or over the telephone. Occasionally you must meet someone face to face. Then you have to look professional, too. You have to look at least as good as your business card and letterhead.

I once worked with a very successful PR agent. No matter where we were—at the studio, on location, even in a war zone—he always dressed impeccably. I complimented him on that one day and he told me it was the result of his first big break in the business. His first big client was Clark Gable. Before hiring him, Gable set down his requirements. "If you're going to work for me," he said, "always dress well and tip big."

So my advice is: Always present yourself professionally. Maybe the other person will pick up the check and leave the tip.

RESPECT YOUR CONTRACTS

It's a myth that writers are always late in delivering their manuscripts. If it's not, it should be. At least in your case.

Professionals honor their contracts, written or oral. Work as hard as you can to deliver your text on time. If you can't, you owe the buyer either an explanation or a warning that delivery may be delayed.

Deliver the size article that you agreed to deliver. If an editor wants a thousand words, send a thousand words. Sure, you might be so fascinated with your research and the slant you've taken that you can write 3,500 words with no trouble, but the editor can't use that many, and certainly doesn't want the added work of trimming 2,500 words out of your piece.

Besides, writing to the proper length shows professional respect for your own writing. If an editor must cut an inordinate amount from your manuscript, the final copy will reflect the editor's style of writing more than yours. If you want your piece to look, feel and sound like your writing, submit the amount of words you agreed to submit.

Also, the finished manuscript should be exactly what the proposal said it would be. Once I worked for four hours with two freelance television writers, polishing the outline for a story line they submitted. When it was completed to everyone's satisfaction, I gave them a go-ahead on the first draft. That meant they walked out of the office that day with a promise of at least $8,500.

When they delivered the first draft of the teleplay two weeks later, it didn't look anything like the outline we had worked on. I made corrections, notes, and mostly filled the margins of the manuscript with giant question marks. Then I called the writers in for a conference.

Again, we referred to the original outline and tried to redirect the script back to that concept—the one I bought. They came back with a second draft that was even more bizarre and further afield than the first.

The Writers Guild rules state that after two drafts, the freelance writer's work is finished. As far as I was concerned, these two writers were. Their two drafts were totally useless, so our writing staff had to rewrite the show from the original outline. The freelancers were paid for their work as contracted, but they would never be invited to a story conference on this show again.

An editor, producer or publisher buys your work based on your presentation. You, as a professional, should deliver, to the best of your ability, what you presented.

TREAT EVERYONE WITH RESPECT

My daughter runs my office. She handles PR, advertising, negotiating, research—just about anything that needs doing. I only step in when there's credit to be taken.

It's a foolproof arrangement because if she works hard and well, she'll make me rich and famous. If she doesn't, she's out of the will. I can't lose.

It also has been enlightening for me, though, because most people calling my office don't realize she's my daughter. They assume she's "just a secretary." Some of them treat her with a rudeness and an arrogance that is unforgivable.

Believe me, this is not an overprotective father speaking. I need much more protection and care than any of my children do. No, I'd be offended at this disrespect regardless who was answering the phone or dealing with this client.

Earlier we said that professionalism was really being considerate, but it's not just being considerate of the "biggies." It's being considerate of all the people you deal with, from the receptionist to the CEO.

Besides, it's just plain good business. Sometimes the person answering the phone is the real power. Often they can get more done for you than the CEO can. I know my daughter is the real power in my office. If you don't believe me, call and ask her.

As a television producer, I used to assemble writing staffs. My decision was usually based on audition scripts. I'd read many writing samples and decide on the best. Before making the final decision, though, my partner and I insisted on a face-to-face meeting. We used to call it our "Two Heads Meeting." We wanted to meet this writer in person to assure ourselves that he wasn't an ogre with two heads. That meant that he wasn't a person who was so obnoxious that he would inhibit the work of the other writers on staff.

To move your career ahead, be professional. Don't have two heads.

CHAPTER 22

TELL THE WORLD YOU'RE READY TO MOVE UP

When I worked in industry, our company once hired a motivational speaker to inspire us to work to our potential and beyond. This gentleman said, "The thing I hate to hear most from salesmen is 'we don't sell much of that item because we don't get much call for it.' Certainly you don't get much call for it because you're not telling people you have it."

He went on: "If you run a furniture store and I ask how many haircuts you gave last week, you're going to say, 'We don't get much call for haircuts.' That's a perfectly valid answer because you're running a furniture store and you don't get much call for haircuts in a furniture store. But I guarantee if you put a barber pole outside that store with those red and white stripes spiraling around, some fool is going to come into your store, sit down in one of those overstuffed chairs, turn to you and say, 'Just trim a little off the back, please, and leave the sideburns.' "

His point was: If you tell enough people that you offer a service or a product, some of them will want it. But you have to tell them.

You've seen the effectiveness of this yourself. You buy a shirt and the salesperson asks, "Would you like to see some ties that would go nicely with that?" "Yes," you say, "I would," even though you had no thought of buying another tie when you went in the store. You buy a new pair of shoes and the salesperson suggests a purse that matches them perfectly. You buy it because she told you she had it.

You as a writer can't assume that editors will come to you and plead for you to write more pieces for their magazine. You can't sit in your writer's space at home and wait for publishers to suggest book proposals to you. You can't expect that other writers will say, "Hey, take your career and move several steps ahead of me."

It's your career that you want to get moving. Tell the writing world that you're ready, willing and able to progress to the next plateau. You must initiate the moves. You must spark people to your potential. Let the industry know that the position it's assigned to you is slightly lower than the position you want and deserve. Put the barber pole outside of your office.

Following are a few ways that you might accomplish this.

MAKE SUGGESTIONS

Be bold. Suggest changes or improvements that are normally made by people who are already in the position you want to be. Go through channels, certainly—no boss will appreciate your going over her head or behind her back—but be innovative.

If you're a newspaper writer, recommend a column that would be popular that you could write. If you've written pieces for a magazine, suggest follow-up articles or a repeating column. If you've done many columns, propose a book.

This serves two purposes. First, the suggestion may be implemented, and you may be assigned the writing of it or the responsibility for it. Second, if enough of your recommendations are worthwhile, the powers that be may recognize your perceptive views and offer you the job you're after.

Let me tell you about a suggestion that I made and reluctantly followed up on.

I was working on a Bob Hope special and I didn't quite understand the premise of the show. I didn't feel the basic idea had enough to support an entire show, so I suggested to Mr. Hope that we at least have a musical production number that defined the show.

He said, "I think you're right. Write one."

I said, "I don't really do musical numbers. Why don't you hire some songwriters?"

He said, "Just give it a try. We'll work on it together."

So I came up with an idea that he liked and I began writing the lyrics. To keep the meter of the lyrics I had to invent a little melody. I sang the ditty to Mr. Hope and he liked it. I called on another of our writers to help me make a few changes, and together we completed the song—lyrics, melody and all. Then the musical director of the show did a complete arrangement, making some adjustments to the lyrics and the melody in the process.

The final number was sung by Mr. Hope, Tony Randall and a choral background. Those of us who worked on the song were nominated for an Emmy for Best Original Song.

We didn't win, but as the cliché goes, a nomination is as good as a win. And this entire adventure was born out of a suggestion.

VOLUNTEER FOR THE POSITION YOU WANT

Again, put up that barber pole. Let people know you have a service or a product available, even if it means some extra work for you. Just because there's an opening available doesn't mean that you're automatically being considered for it—even if you're the most deserving candidate. Actually, you're not a candidate at all until the people who make the assignment consider you a candidate. It's quite possible they could overlook you. But they can't if you remind them that you're there.

Walk into their offices with the barber pole in your hands if you must.

WRITE PIECES ON SPEC

One way to move up to the next plateau is to write pieces that the next plateau demands—on spec. On spec, of course, means for no guaranteed salary or sale. It means writing as a gamble or to prove to yourself and to others that you can write at that level.

When I was writing for television I talked with my agent about his getting me some commitments in film. He kept discouraging me. "You're a funny variety show writer," he'd say. (Remember we talked about the scourge of the pigeonhole earlier?)

I said, "At least mention my name to some film producers. They might want to see some of my product."

He said, "You're established in television. Let's capitalize on that."

Finally I wrote a screenplay—on spec. I did a 140-page script, which I sent to my agent.

"It didn't knock me on my butt," he said.

I said, "Show it to film producers."

He said, "It's too long. I can't show them 140 pages. Cut twenty pages from it."

I cut the twenty pages.

He said, "It's not the kind of story they're buying."

I said, "Show it to somebody."

He said, "You're a television writer."

I said, "Show it to somebody."

Finally, more to shut me up than anything else, he sent it to a film producer that he played racquetball with. The producer agreed to read it more as a favor than anything else.

Then the producer called after reading the screenplay and set up a meeting with me. He liked the script, but had some changes he wanted to discuss. The deal began to develop.

During these discussions and negotiations, my television contract came up for renewal. My agent said to the producers, "I think we'll have to discuss major changes in the contract because Gene's primarily a film writer now."

I could have talked to my agent and countless producers forever, promoting myself and my screenwriting abilities, but nothing would have convinced them. A hundred and twenty pages convinced them for me.

All of us have trouble selling our potential as writers, and that's understandable because all of us feel we are the greatest writer on the face of the earth. We all feel that our book has best-seller potential. We all believe we're future candidates for the Pulitzer Prize. The buyers have heard it all before. They know that all of us can talk a good game.

If you firmly believe you have that kind of potential, put it on paper. Let your manuscript be your salesperson.

ASK

It may sound simplistic, but if there's something you want, ask for it. The worst that can happen is that you'll get "no" for an answer. However, you might get "yes" and be on your way.

I admonish young comedy writers to do just that—ask many comedians if they'd like to buy their wares. I did that when I was first peddling my one-liners. Many, many, *many* of the comics said "no." Phyllis Diller said "yes," and I had a career going. That's the nice thing about asking: one "yes" can nullify a bunch of "no's."

In review, I find that most of the jobs I got in television, magazines and publishing resulted from asking. Usually I asked, the buyer said "yes," and the agent stepped in to complete the details.

You'll probably discover that most of your writing sales result from asking, too. A query letter is nothing more than asking if the editor would be interested in this piece you'd like to write. A book proposal is a request.

Now, if you have some direction you want your career to move in, or some position you want, ask.

ASK AGAIN

You won't always get a positive reply when you ask. I know, because my brother asked my dad every Christmas and probably two or three other times during the year if we could have a pony. He asked that from the time he first knew what a pony was until he was old enough to realize that owning a pony in a row home in South Philadelphia would be impossible. The most he ever got was a cocker spaniel.

Editors won't always spark to your request. They won't always feel that the article you suggest is right for their magazine. Publishers won't always agree that your book of poetry will have enormous sales potential. Sometimes they won't agree that the short filler you sent to them is worth five dollars.

Often you'll get a flat, reverberating, incontestable "no." Sometimes you'll get a weak "maybe." But ask again. Keep reminding them that you're there and that you have considerable talent and a drive to move ahead. Sooner or later, they'll acknowledge either your talent or your persistence. You don't care which, so long as you get where you're going.

When I was a youngster in ponyless South Philadelphia I used to sit on the front step and hum to myself. The humming was hardly audible to my own ear and I'm sure no passersby heard it. Yet I daydreamed that some Hollywood producer would wander by and say to me, "Hey, you sing pretty well. How'd you like to come to Hollywood and become the next Frank Sinatra? You'll star in movies, make records, appear in nightclubs, and make several million dollars a year. Whatd'ya say? D'ya wanna do it? You'd better make up your mind. You're ten years old; you don't have forever."

No Hollywood producers ever came down my street. No one ever offered to make me the next Frank Sinatra. It was a childish fantasy.

No one is going to offer to make you the next Scott Turow or Danielle Steel. No producer will wonder down your street and turn you into Sylvester Stallone or Mel Brooks.

You must let the industry know you're a good writer and that you're ready to move onward and upward.

CHAPTER 23

PROMOTE YOURSELF

I was invited to a party during one of my visits to my family on the East Coast. In casual conversation with several of the other guests, someone asked what I did. I told them I was a writer — a comedy writer. For some unexplained reason, this annoyed one of the guests.

He began to pick on me, referring to me as "the wise guy," "the funny guy," or, worse yet, "the guy who thinks he's funny." Throughout the evening he kept challenging me to "say something funny."

I didn't bother responding because I knew this boor would bury himself sooner or later. Finally, he did. He asked me, loudly enough for most of the party to hear, "So tell me, who do you write this comedy for? Anybody I ever heard of?"

I said, "I don't know. Have you ever heard of Bob Hope? Phyllis Diller? Carol Burnett?" His jaw dropped, which was sweet revenge for me.

However, this chapter's not about revenge. That's a luxury few of us struggling writers can afford anyway. I just got lucky with this loudmouth. But there are lessons in that story for those of us who want to advance our career. Let's analyze it from a more pragmatic point of view.

When I announced my litany of clients, I instantly established credibility. I wasn't just a flunkie who tried his hand at selling a joke or two here and there; I was a writer of some standing in the comedy community. I had been hired by the best, so my work must have some merit.

Notice I didn't furnish samples of my work to anyone. No one there knew if I wrote good jokes or bad. Yet because I wrote for Hope, Diller and Burnett, I was an established comedy writer.

Also, my loutish antagonist wasn't the only one at the party who didn't know what I did for a living. After I made my dramatic (and admittedly spiteful) announcement, though, everyone knew.

Suppose the next day someone happened to say to one of these people who had been at the party, "You know, I'm looking for a good comedy writer." Chances are that person, who hardly knew me, would say, "Hey, I know about a guy who's a pretty good comedy writer. Why don't you give him a call?"

So my revenge-motivated self-promotion established my credibility; it got me known by a wider circle of people; and it also either informed or reminded people that I was in the business of selling comedy material. It also got people to network for me—to do some of my promoting for me.

That's what self-promotion can do for your career, too.

ESTABLISH CREDIBILITY

Most of the writing sales I've seen have not been made by material, but by reputation. If you've never written a novel before and you set out to study the craft, outline a magnificent story and write it expertly, you'll still have trouble selling that novel to a publisher. However, if Stephen King says, "I would like to write a novel about . . . " some publishing house will offer him a seven-figure advance before one word is typed on a page.

They know Stephen King's work. His work is dependable, it's popular and it sells. He has established his credibility in the fiction field.

Buyers rely on past history. It's easier to get a second novel purchased if you've already written a first one. It's easier to get a novel published if your first novel was a success. Success builds on success, not only in writing, but in most fields. So it pays to capitalize on whatever success you enjoy. Promote yourself shamelessly. Tell the world that you've written, tell them what you've written, and tell them what you're capable of writing.

EXPAND YOUR UNIVERSE

The "universe," in marketing terms, is the potential number of buyers for your product. For instance, if you sell bumper stickers that say "I Am a Former President of the United States," your universe may total four. If you sell bumper stickers that say "Baby on Board," the universe expands dramatically to all those drivers who are parents. If you sell bumper stickers that read "I'd Rather Be Driving a Car That's Paid For," you might sell to everyone who lives in the United States.

Some writers' careers may stall because they've saturated their universe. They have to reach out to new markets or new buyers.

When I was a kid I always dreamed of winning the bicycle that was offered as a prize to whoever sold the most subscriptions to a magazine. I never won it. After I sold to my parents, my older brothers and sisters (if they were in a generous mood), and a few aunts and uncles, my universe was exhausted. Five subscriptions was not going to win the new Schwinn. No, that award went to someone who sold hundreds or thousands of subscriptions. Those dynamic salespeople attacked a much broader market. They widened their universe. I was much more comfortable having Mom buy a magazine she didn't want. Aunt Rose and Aunt Sally might part with two bucks for their nephew, too. Those sales were easy for me. I didn't have to knock on strangers' doors or huckster the magazines on the street.

Sometimes we writers become comfortable with our universe, too. We have a few magazines who will buy our articles, a few editors that trust us. We may not be totally happy with the income we derive from this "family," but we're satisfied with it.

Self-promotion, though, might expand that universe. It can tell more people about our work and our availability.

KEEP YOUR NAME CURRENT

Earlier I mentioned that people who were at that party would have gladly referred me to anyone who was looking for a comedy writer. After all, how many comedy writers do you know? If you knew of one, wouldn't you recommend him?

However, that would only apply the following morning. If someone asked them even a month later, they'd probably respond, "Off the top of my head, I don't know a one."

People forget.

Sometimes, even though a writer establishes dependability and credibility, the marketplace can forget her. Self-promotion can remind those people that she's around, working and available.

People tend to trust names they've heard of, too. I was once being considered for a speaking engagement. My major competition was an ex-football player. He was a damned good football player, but I could cut rings around him on the podium. He hadn't had enough experience on the speaking circuit to be very polished. The people doing the hiring knew that, too. They had audition tapes of both of us. Yet he was hired at twice the fee that I would have gotten. Why? Because people knew his name.

That's not sour grapes on my part; those are the facts of life on the speaking circuit. Ollie North can ask for — and get — five figures for one speaking engagement because people know his name. Through self-promotion, people can know your name, too. Keep it circulating. Keep it current.

Self-promotion has other fringe benefits, too. When I was working in industry, I was the emcee at most of the employee functions: retirement parties, going-away parties, twenty-five-year ceremonies and such. I gained a companywide reputation as a humorous speaker.

However, I found at the same time that I was being considered for many promotions available around the plant. Why? Because the people on these committees were usually in the audience when I emceed, so my name popped into their heads. I didn't always get the promotion, of course, but I was on the list.

That's a tremendous benefit for a writer, to always be on "the list," to have editors think of you when they need writing.

Self-promotion can help accomplish that for you.

KEEP NETWORKING

I'm always amazed and flattered when I meet another writer who knows about me and my work. Generally, when I ask how they heard of me, they'll say, "Oh, so-and-so told me about you." (Of course, I usually know all about the other writer from speaking to friends of mine who know *her* work.)

There is a subculture of networking that exists. It's like a pyramid effect. A person who knows and admires your work may tell a few friends. Those people will tell other people, and theoretically, on and on ad infinitum.

Consequently, the more people who know about you and your work, the farther this networking effect extends. Whatever self-promotion you do will send off concentric circles, like ripples in a lake, circulating to a much wider audience.

Self-promotion has many benefits for the writer. Some of them are immediate, some long term. Many are obvious, a few hidden. Following are a few suggestions for your own promotion program.

WORD OF MOUTH

Tell people what you do and what you hope to do. Tell relatives, friends, strangers — anybody who will listen. When you do, you enlist a whole squadron of promoters to help you with your career. Somebody may know somebody who knows somebody who knows somebody's brother who can do you some good.

I owe my career to this process. As I mentioned, I had some notoriety as a company humorist. I told coworkers that I would like to write professionally, to sell material to comedians. One person told her dad, who used to be a musician. He knew a local comedian who'd had some success in Hollywood but still worked locally. He called this comic and set up a meeting. We met and I brought along some of my gags. He couldn't use them, but he recommended me to a local television personality who was considering my ghost-writing a newspaper column for him. The column never happened, but another comedian guested on his show, saw my material, gave me a call, and signed me to a writing contract. That was my first professional gig, my start. It came from telling a friend.

Be honest, though. Exaggerating your successes or lying about your accomplishments can backfire. And magnifying your career isn't necessary. In fact, it can be detrimental. You want others to help you, to promote you. If you paint a picture of outrageous success, they might figure, "Why bother?"

Once when I spoke at a luxurious resort, I brought my teenage daughter along—to enjoy a short vacation and also to hear my talk. I warned her that at the cocktail party that evening I would be busy meeting people and answering questions, so I couldn't constantly entertain her. She would have to socialize on her own. Then at the party, I overheard a slight bit of her conversation. One man said to her, "It must be quite a thrill for you, having a dad who works with Bob Hope and Tim Conway and people like that." She said dryly, "Oh, is he still telling people that?"

I got strange looks from many of the party-goers the rest of the evening. They were trying to discern whether I was really the fraud my daughter jokingly pretended me to be.

So be honest; it's easier.

TELL THE PRESS

You're much more interesting than you think you are. Really—and so is your work. Newspapers and magazines may be interested in what you do, what you know, and what you hope to do someday. Your accomplishments don't have to be major front-page news stories. The papers often look for softer pieces: human-interest, people-oriented stories.

I once suggested a story to a magazine, which wrote back asking what type of printer I used to generate the copy. I wrote back and told them. They were interested in what kind of equipment I had in my home office. They sent a reporter and a photographer to do an article about the office in my home and the computer hardware and software I used. That I was a writer was almost an aside, but it was mentioned in the article.

The papers don't have to be the majors, either. Your local paper may be interested, as may the in-house magazine or newsletter where you work. Does your old school have an alumni bulletin? Maybe its editor would publish something about your work.

Some writers may feel timid about such blatant self-promotion. There's no need to. It's a win-win situation. The editors of such publications often look for local angles. Yours may be perfect for them. If it's not, they won't publish it.

The old saying is that there's no such thing as bad press so long as they spell your name right. Well, I'm not sure that's totally true, but it *does* pay to get some mentions of your work, even if they're in the smaller, local papers or periodicals. Again, such exposure can have far-reaching effects that we can never visualize or imagine. One article can lead to another one in a different periodical. Someone can read the article and contact you about something totally unrelated to what the story was about. Who knows?

Your librarian can help you find a listing of all the newspapers and periodicals in print, and also a listing of syndicated columnists.

WRITE ARTICLES

You also can get your name in print as a byline. Write about what you do, about your profession. You don't have to be an expert and your articles don't need to be instructional. I've seen articles by young comedians who haven't made it in the comedy field talking about their failures, about the struggles to make it. Do a collection of helpful hints for organizing and running a home office. Talk about your first sale, your first interview, your first whatever. Heck, you're a creative writer; you can come up with some slant.

The beauty of this is that at the end of each article, most magazines will put a little descriptive bio: "Jane Doe is a successful writer living in Anywhere, USA." Another form of self-promotion.

A comedy writer friend of mine has been hitting the op-ed page of the newspapers. He gives a little humorous slant to whatever makes the big headlines on the front page. Again, the short article has a little descriptive phrase at the end telling the world that he writes material for some major comedians.

GUEST ON RADIO TALK SHOWS (WITHOUT LEAVING YOUR HOUSE)

There are countless radio talk and call-in shows around the country. They're hungry for interesting guests, and many of them will interview you on the phone. I can't tell you how many times I've talked to listeners from far-away states while sitting comfortably in my home office in my pajamas and slippers while my wife stopped in periodically to freshen my morning coffee. It's fun, it's easy, and it's publicity for your writing.

How do you get such gigs? Write to various stations outlining your credentials. Tell them what you write about and how you can interest their listeners. You don't need extensive credits or celebrity status: If you've written, you've most likely done research; if you've done research, you're probably more knowledgeable than most of the listeners. Offer that expertise to the radio station. Your knowledge becomes even more appealing to programmers if it ties in with some current news topic. For example, if you've researched and written articles about drought, you might be welcome on a radio talk show in southern California. However, you must let the shows know your qualifications and availability.

Your local library can help you find a listing of radio stations nationwide, or you can subscribe to publications like Bacon's

Radio/TV Directory (332 South Michigan Avenue, Chicago, IL 60604).

Or, for a fee, you can even place a notice in publications such as these:

The Radio/TV Interview Report
Bradley Communications Corp.
135 E. Plumstead Ave.
P.O. Box 1206
Lansdowne, PA 19050

Broadcast Interview Source
2233 Wisconsin Ave., NW
Washington, DC 20007-4104

Talkout
(Professional Broadcaster's Guide to
Talk Show Guests)
Authors National Service Bureau
P.O. Box 201601
Austin, TX 78720-1601

GET ON TELEVISION

You will have to leave the house for this — and change into something less comfortable than your bathrobe.

Most cities have at least one magazine-type television show that you can use to promote yourself. Write its producers a captivating, but honest, query letter. Spell out your credentials, your credits, and what you can bring to their viewing audience.

Also, query the major network shows. They're harder to get on, but they're worth a try. You may not have a big enough reputation yet to be one of their major guests, but you might fit into some sort of theme show they have planned. You never know.

I heard of one story where a man's children wrote to Oprah Winfrey with an ingenuous request. Their dad's birthday was approaching and they wanted to get him his fifteen minutes of fame on television. Would the show consider him as a guest? Sounds naive, right?

The show wrote back and asked what one of his secret dreams might be. Why? Because they had decided to do a show about fulfilling secret dreams. This man not only guested on the show, but danced with a celebrity — that was his dream.

Promote yourself every chance you get and in any way you can (but keep it reasonable and legal). Remember, it's your career, so you have to let the world, or at least the industry, know that you're available. You'll be surprised — if you just keep reminding the buyers that you're there and own a word processor, your career will start zooming.

CHAPTER 24

DEMOTE YOURSELF

Demote yourself. It appears to be the opposite of *pro*mote your-self, but it really isn't. Like the general said, "We're not retreat-ing; we're just fighting in the opposite direction." Demoting yourself in this context is promoting yourself in the opposite direction.

By demoting yourself, I mean to do those things that you've outgrown, that are bothersome, that don't pay enough, that seem to have no potential. Humble yourself occasionally and do a few of these chores. You needn't overburden yourself with them, but once in a while they can not only be fun, they can be beneficial.

Let me give you an example. As I've mentioned, I gained some localized celebrity as an after-dinner speaker where I worked. I was trying to capitalize on this, use it as a stepping-stone to the next plateau of my career. I tried to convince a local television personality that he should do a monologue to open his show and I was the one to write it for him. However, I wasn't having much luck setting up a meeting with him to discuss my idea.

Then a friend asked if I would do a favor for her friend: give a luncheon talk to a nearby women's club. I didn't want to do it because I was getting cocky. I wanted to go to Hollywood and entertain millions, not a few miles down the Baltimore Pike to entertain thirty-five or forty women at a luncheon. But I went.

I did pretty well, and the next day the local television star called me. We had our meeting and I wrote some audition material for him. It never led to writing monologue material for his show, but it did lead to some other contracts that helped further my writing career.

Why did he call? His wife was the president of the club that I addressed. She was the friend of the friend that I did the favor for. When she mentioned my speech to her husband and gave me a good review, he recognized the name and thought, "What the hell, I'll give him a call."

What in my estimation was demoting myself turned out to be promoting my career. So occasionally it pays to work "beneath your station in life." Give a talk on creative writing to the fifth-grade class at your local school and have a generous question-and-answer period with the youngsters. You'll find they're fascinated and they'll ask probing questions. They'll enjoy it almost as much as you will.

Offer a short writing course to a local group of senior citizens. Write an article for little or no pay for some periodical that you believe in. Volunteer on-air commentary for local public radio or public-access television. These stations have plenty of air time to fill with quality material, but little or no money. Many influential people pay attention to their broadcasts, though.

Do something for which you must give more than you get in return. You might find that you get more in return than you expected. Of course, it's not magical. Not every assignment like this will lead to bigger and better things. Some will just be loads of fun. Others will just be headaches and bothers. You can't predict. You have to be like the miner panning for gold. You pick up a panful of dirt and swirl it around carefully, looking for those gleaming particles that can add up to a worthwhile payoff.

Some of them can be beneficial. Once in a great while, one can be a career-maker. If you dismiss all of them as beneath you, you'll never find the gold hidden in them.

Here are some benefits these adventures can have for you.

THEY CAN BROADEN YOUR OUTLOOK

Writing is a private occupation, and it seems the more successful you become, the more isolated you become. In the beginning you have a day job to pay your bills and you work in your free time. Then you enjoy some sales and some success and you designate a room or corner of your house as your office, your writing space. Should you become successful enough to live off your writing, that small room or corner becomes your world. You spend hours there, meeting only the characters you create. You have exchanges with more mythical people than real people.

Your professional universe compacts also. If you've become a successful writer of Western novels, for example, you begin to think entirely about the Old West and relate all of your experiences to cowboys and Indians. You become narrow-minded.

I once took my brother, who was visiting from the East Coast, to a Hollywood party. It was a birthday party for a comedy writer and most of the guests were television producers or writers. Afterward, I asked my brother how he enjoyed himself. He said, "It was fun, but you folks never talk about anything but show business."

I said, "Well, that's our profession. That's what we do for a living."

He said, "Well, I work with computers, but when we have a party we sometimes talk about sports or the weather."

My brother was right. We had grown smaller as writers. We lived in a world all our own. It was a world that excluded everything outside of television production. We even reduced major world events to either monologue material or premises for situation comedies.

Accepting some assignments that are outside the normal range of your writing profession can help broaden your outlook. It can open your eyes to the rest of the world. That can only benefit your writing.

There's a joke about a television executive who constantly commutes back and forth from New York to California. On one flight, he's forced to take a window seat on the plane. Somewhere over Kansas, he glances down, slaps his head in surprise, and says, "My God, there are people living down there."

Television thinks that everyone is in the industry and everyone lives either in New York or Los Angeles. They slant their shows to those people. Isn't the better executive the one who realizes that people also live in Idaho, Iowa, Kansas, and all the rest of the forty-eight states besides New York and California? Isn't the better show the one that reaches *all* the people?

THEY GET YOU OUT OF YOUR CLOISTER

These assignments, too, get you out of your office, away from your keyboard, off your duff, and out meeting people.

Sid Caesar on his old television show once did a take-off of *On the Waterfront*, the Marlon Brando blockbuster movie. A major plot point in that film was that the street people were supposed to be "D and D"—"deaf and dumb," which meant they weren't supposed to rat on the gangsters that controlled the waterfront.

Sid Caesar, playing the punch-drunk boxer that Marlon Brando portrayed in the film, said to his gangster brother, "Charlie, I always done what you told me. I was always D and D, Charlie. I was deaf and dumb. I never said nothing to nobody, Charlie. D and D, Charlie. I never talked to nobody. You told me never to talk to nobody, Charlie, so I was D and D. I never talked to nobody. Although, I think you were wrong, Charlie. I think you should have let me talk to Mom and Dad. They were nice folks, Charlie, and I never got to know them."

Writers can be D and D, too. We write about people, so we should get out and meet them occasionally. I mean, meet people who aren't writers or publishers or editors or agents.

"Demoting" ourselves out of the writing arena can get us out of our cloister. It can help us meet other charming, interesting people.

THEY CAN EXPAND YOUR UNIVERSE

Meeting new people always exposes us to new opportunities. As I mentioned earlier, I met a hard-to-reach client by delivering a humorous speech to a group that his wife belonged to. I used to address the local fifth-grade writing class and the high-school journalism students each year. Many times, I've gone to business meetings and had someone say to me, "I know you. My kid really enjoyed your talk at the school."

A few years ago my niece persuaded me to visit her college journalism class for a question-and-answer period. It was a favor that she asked desperately; her grade needed the extra credit of delivering a live speaker to the class.

The professor turned out to be a successful magazine writer who also organized writer's seminars for Reader's Digest. He asked if I'd consider speaking and teaching at one of these seminars—for expenses only.

I agreed to that because it sounded like fun and some writing exposure. Since then, I've been on many trips with this faculty, which includes editors not only from the *Digest*, but also from many of the most respected magazines in the country. On these trips we're usually wined and dined by the local chambers of commerce or hotels, we have a great time together, and we enjoy exchanges with interested writers. But also, I've gained friends in the writing profession and have sold many articles and books as a direct result of contacts I've made through these seminars.

Of course, not every one of these adventures has led to sales, or even good times. Many of them are frustrating, disappointing, and hard work with no return. Those, though, you can chalk up to experience, which is a benefit, too.

However, as a writer who is interested in progressing, you should not dismiss these "demotions." They have potential; they can help to move your career forward if you give them a chance.

CHAPTER 25

REVIEW AND *ANALYZE* THE *MARKETS YOU ALREADY HAVE*

I went to a Little League game once. Well, it wasn't really Little League; it was tee-ball. The youngsters were hardly big enough to hit or throw the ball and certainly not old enough to understand the game. They hit the ball off a stand-up tee, hence the name.

One lad dribbled the ball off the tee and scrambled to first base. He was safe; most of them were.

The next batter belted the ball pretty well. Hard enough to reach the infielders, anyway. The defensive players scrambled for the ball and tossed it every which way. No one could catch it.

The batter zoomed around first, turned second, headed for third. He didn't care where the ball or the fielders were; he was just going to keep running. Somebody threw the ball somewhere and the lad dashed home, and slid across the plate. The slide was unnecessary because no one knew where the ball was.

It was a perfect "inside the infield" home run, except for one thing. The other runner was still standing on first base.

The coach said, "Why didn't you run?"

The boy said, "This was the first time I ever got on first base. I didn't want to leave it."

This boy had a good thing in his young life, and he wasn't going to abandon it.

The writing business can be similar to running those bases. You use your talent to get to first base, which gives you the opportunity to reach second base, which allows you to go to third, which enables you to try for home.

Success in writing is built on credits. Each sale theoretically makes the next sale easier. If you've written several magazine articles, other editors are more inclined to buy from you. If you've sold short stories, you've got a better chance of selling your first novel. If you've published good-selling novels, you're in a better position to sell a screenplay. You use your past sales as stepping-stones to your next sales.

At each step along the way you meet people who can help your progress. My mom used to say frequently: "It's not what you know, but who you know." It was a sour-grapes comment that was only partially true. Who you know is important, but what Mom overlooked was that it's what you know (or how good you are at doing what you do) that determines who you know.

With each sale you make, you'll meet influential people: an editor, a producer, a buyer. Someone in authority must have been impressed by your work to have purchased it.

Beginning comedy writers that I work with often ask, "How do I know if someone likes my jokes or not?" The answer is, "If they send you a check for them, they like them."

Make a list of the publications you've sold to already. These are organizations that like your work; they've paid you for it.

The writing industry is structured on confidence. You'll understand better if you look at the process from the buyer's point of view. As a television producer, I listened to countless writers at pitch sessions—meetings where freelance writers talk to producers about their story ideas, with the hopes of selling a script.

When we liked a premise, we would work with those writers to develop a workable outline, and then give them the go-ahead.

"You've made the sale," we'd say. "Now be back in two weeks with your first draft."

If these were new writers, we never knew what to expect. Sometimes they'd change the entire outline without consulting us, thinking, of course, that they were improving it. Occasionally they'd keep the outline intact, but the writing would be inferior. Sometimes the writers would deliver a first draft that was right on the nose, exactly what we wanted, and with only minor fixes required. Those are the writers we wanted to use again.

It's easier for the buyer if she knows the writer's work and has confidence in it. Deadlines can be tighter. Other work related to this project can be started without fear. For instance, if this is a teleplay, sets can be built. If it's an article, photographs can be assigned.

Remember, you have a much better opportunity of selling to an organization that already trusts your talent.

Make a list of people you've worked with, too. Everything we said above about organizations applies to individuals. In a sense, it might apply more. An editor's lifeblood is his writers. I'm always fascinated, in talking to magazine editors, at how they adopt writers. They speak of them as "my" writers. They take great pride in having developed these authors and trained them well enough to become part of their stable.

If you're one of those writers, you have a valuable ally. Those allies, though, are only beneficial if you use them.

Also, the worlds of publishing, television and films change constantly. Whoever produced this show last year is producing that show this year. The producers of last year's hit movie are now searching for this year's blockbusters. Editors that worked for this magazine or book publisher have moved on to that periodical or publishing house. By maintaining contact with individuals—editors, producers, publishers—you broaden your marketing base.

If an editor at *Magazine A* likes and buys your work, you have two marketing contacts: the editor and the magazine. If that editor moves on to *Magazine B*, you can now sell to both

Magazine A and *Magazine B*. Most likely, you'll gain a new ally: the new editor you work with at *Magazine A*.

So if you call and discover that "Oh, Ms. So-and-So no longer works here," don't be disappointed. Ask two questions: "Who has taken over her editorial duties?" and "Can you tell me where I might reach Ms. So-and-So?"

If the editors you work with move upward, that can create new opportunities for you. If they move laterally, that can still broaden your marketing base.

How can maintaining contact with these organizations and individuals benefit your career?

1. You can move your career to a higher level, or at least expand it if they move laterally.
2. You can sell to them again.
3. You can use them for research.
4. You can use them for recommendations.

MOVE YOUR CAREER TO A HIGHER LEVEL

If you establish a dependable working relationship with a company or individual, use this as a springboard to higher levels. It's a normal workaday process. Periodically, a worker goes in and asks the boss for a raise. The worker either gets it or doesn't.

You, the writer, are entitled to do the same thing—ask for an upgrade. Now those upgrades can be any number of things, depending on what sort of writing you do, and how imaginative you are. But let's look at a couple of examples.

If you're a writer who creates captions for cartoonists and you've had success with one artist, you might suggest doing a book together.

If you're an essayist who has regularly sold columns to a certain newspaper, you might suggest a regular column and possible syndication.

Whatever type of writing you do, you can probably come up with other innovative upgrades of your own.

Will you always get what you asked for? Certainly not. But

you might get *something* you ask for. And there are other variations, as well.

Your request may not be one they would consider, but it might inspire them to think of other applications for your talent. For instance, the cartoonist may nix the book idea but suggest that you work on a regular monthly retainer, rather than on a freelance basis, in exchange for getting a first look at your ideas. The newspaper may turn down a regular column but ask you to do a series of editorials on a given topic it plans to run.

These examples are hypothetical, but they show that when you take the initiative with people who trust your work, it can lead to other rewards that you haven't even thought of. In my own career, many of the assignments I enjoyed resulted directly from suggesting ideas to people I had already worked with. My first salaried contract was because I asked a comic I had been working with to put me on a retainer rather than a freelance basis. My first staff job in television was because I asked a comic who was starting a television show if I could write the opening monologues. My first book was sold because I asked a publisher who was familiar with my joke-writing if I might try a humorous book for his company.

I believe in this principle because I've seen it work.

SELL TO THEM AGAIN

If people paid for your work, they liked it. If they liked it, they'll pay for it again. So contact them.

Writers say, "Wait a minute. If they like me and my work so much, why don't they come to me?" As we discussed in chapter one, it's your career. It's up to you to do the marketing. That's like a homeowner saying, "If people want to buy my house, why don't they come knock on the door and ask about it? Why do I have to put a 'For Sale' sign out on the lawn?"

You have to remind people of your talent.

Let me show you another reason why you must prompt them to take action. I worked with one editor for several months on two or three projects that his publishing company had bought.

As I spoke with him on the phone, I would visualize his office. It was a Hollywood image. I pictured a spacious office, elegantly appointed with a huge imposing desk, paneled walls, and shelves of books neatly arranged.

Then one day I visited New York and met with this editor. His office was a cubbyhole. It had a desk, but I couldn't tell you what it was made of because it was covered with manuscripts, letters and books. There was a small bookcase, but the books weren't neatly arranged. They were crammed onto the shelves any way they would fit.

The editor had to move books off of the one visitor's chair onto the floor so that I could sit during our meeting. Each time he searched for a document or book to show me, it would be under a towering pile of other documents just as important. When he pulled one out, others would fall over.

This person had other writers to work with, other books to work on, other documents and reports to read and refer to. This was a busy office, a busy executive.

Most people you work with in the writing industry will be as harried as this. They're overloaded with work and impossible deadlines. If you want to get their attention, you have to seek it.

Another reason you must initiate contact is that some radical rumors may be circulating about you. I've called people I used to work with and got responses such as, "I heard you died" or, "Someone told me you gave up writing and became a shepherd in New Zealand." One person even told me he had heard that he and I were having a feud, so he didn't dare call me. There was absolutely no basis to it, but he thought that I wasn't talking to him, so he didn't talk to me.

Sometimes, too, the buyers might assume that you're too busy to work for them. Just calling to let them know you're available might land you an assignment.

Contact the people you've worked with. Send them ideas, query letters, proposals. If those are turned down, ask what they're in the market for. Then act on those suggestions to generate other ideas that might be more marketable.

I contacted one editor I had worked with in the past with a

suggestion for a book. He turned that proposal down but mailed me his company's "hot list." This was a catalog of the type of books the company wanted to do; books it felt would sell. He asked me to study the catalog and see if there were any books on that list that I might feel qualified to write.

Now if that's not getting the benefit of a past relationship, I don't know what is.

USE THEM FOR RESEARCH

As we noted earlier, the people in the writing industry move around. They meet people and build up contacts. They work with other people in the industry. They hear the scuttlebutt. They know who's who, who does what, and who's looking for what.

You can take advantage of that knowledge. Suppose you're looking for a new agent or an agent who handles a different kind of writing. Who better to recommend some names than the editors or publishers who deal with agents daily? They'll probably know the good ones and the ones who can handle your type of project best. Why not ask?

USE THEM FOR RECOMMENDATIONS

Again, they know the business; they know people in the business. They can tell you where to go and who to ask for. Suppose, for example, you have been writing some fine fiction pieces for one magazine editor, and now you're ready to market your first novel. The magazine's not going to buy it, but this editor may be able to recommend some people in book publishing whom you can contact. That's priceless information.

They might, too, if you ask and if they have the clout, put in a good word for you with those people they recommend. It's worth a shot if it gets your manuscript read.

Then, too, they might offer reverse recommendations. Rather than tell you to search for a market, they might tell a market to search for you. If they know you're now interested in writing novels, they could suggest to an agent or book publisher to give you a call. It has happened before and it will continue to happen, if you initiate the contact.

The markets you already have may be more extensive and far more valuable than you realize. When I first began to work for Phyllis Diller I wanted to send her more material, but I was too timid. "She'll think I'm getting too greedy. She may not be able to afford to buy any more than I'm sending her now. She'll tell me to forget the whole deal if I'm not satisfied with the money I'm already making." Those were the thoughts that kept me from writing and sending more comedy material to her.

When I finally met Ms. Diller backstage after her performance, the first thing she said to me was, "The problem with you, Gene, is that you don't write enough for me."

Lesson learned.

Cultivate the contacts you already have.

CHAPTER 26

MAKE NEW CONTACTS

We speak of the business of writing and we talk about all of the buyers as if they were impersonal entities. We talk of Random House or *McCall's* or Paramount or NBC. However, all of these are staffed by people. Every office in these organizations has a desk and a chair. Why? Because someone has to sit in that chair and do work at that desk. Real people actually work in these places. Random House is people. So is NBC. So are all the rest.

The business of writing is the business of people. You don't sell a book to Random House; you sell to an editor at Random House. You don't sell a show to NBC; you sell to an executive at NBC. *People* buy and sell writing.

One way to expand your business is to expand the number of people in the business that you know.

However, one of the enticements of the writing life is that it's so private, so self-contained. You sit in a room with your keyboard and your imagination and you turn out pages of material that *you* want to write. No one looks over your shoulder. No one tells you what to write or how to rewrite. Only your computer spell-checker corrects your typos. That's nice.

That's part of being a writer. The other part is leaving that office. Writing is not only an art, but a business. The art is rewarding; the business pays the bills. The writer can remain locked in the study; the businessperson has to get out and meet other writers, agents, editors, publishers, producers, entrepreneurs — people in the industry.

I often work the banquet circuit. I've given talks to cranberry growers, turkey farmers, brick manufacturers, pharmacists, nurses, and physicians who specialize in renal disorders. There is an association for everything in the country. Each one holds at least one convention a year, and members flock to it.

Why? Because there are definite benefits. There are the social rewards: You meet people who are interested in the same things you're interested in. There are the business rewards: You learn more about your industry, you can influence and vote on decisions that your industry makes, and you meet people in the profession—potential employers, employees, customers, or allies in your work.

So writers must go where the writers are. In other words, become a part of the writing business. Join writing clubs, become active in writing guilds and associations, and attend seminars and workshops.

I've recently read Writer's Digest Book's *1992 Guide to Literary Agents and Art/Photo Reps*. Each of the articles in the book recommends meeting agents at writers' conferences. If it's not the most frequent way of acquiring an agent, it's close to it.

The other method mentioned in the book is referrals. But again, referrals come from people. People you get to know recommend you to people that they know, and your business expands.

I had a friend who was in the investment business. He was an outgoing person who entertained often. He took people to lunch, invited them to dinner at his house, threw frequent parties and made friends easily. He lived in a community that boasted the number-one per capita income in the state.

When times changed and that community slipped to number two in the ratings, he moved. He entertained and met friends in the community with the new number-one per capita income. When surveys revealed a change later, he moved again. Why? He was going where the money was. He was meeting new people who could invest. His business was money, so he lived, worked and socialized where there was money—big money. That's only common sense.

You want to meet industry people—*powerful* industry people. But if you're not yet among the powerful, how do you get to them?

Again, one way is to go where the powerful people go. Attend workshops or seminars where powerful people speak or teach. If you try to schedule a meeting with a noted agent, you might find that she doesn't have time. Yet, if that same person speaks at a writers' convention, she'll likely schedule informal chats with potential clients or even converse informally with you over the outdoor barbecue.

However, you can also meet or communicate with the power people more directly: through the mail or over the telephone. I have several professional friends—not acquaintances, friends—whom I've never met. I worked with both Phyllis Diller and Bob Hope for many months before I met either one of them. The classic, though, is one man I know who has been a successful television writer now for almost two decades and has never met his agent. They chat on the telephone and send contracts and other documents through the mail or over the fax, but they've never shaken hands and said hello face to face.

Many people—powerful people—are more approachable than you would imagine. Some aren't. There are curmudgeons in every business. There's no harm, though, in taking the initiative. Write or call.

One caveat, though: These are busy, professional people. Your communications should reflect that, which simply means "professional courtesy." Like all courtesy, that's mostly common sense.

Let's discuss mail courtesy first.

Write Without Asking for Something

Remember that not all of your letters have to be supplications. You're not limited to writing only when you have a problem or a question that needs answering. You can write to wish a person well, or to compliment that person on a job well done.

Celebrities and powerful people in the industry are basically still human beings. When they do a good job at whatever they do, they don't mind being complimented.

Let me give you an example that deals with a face-to-face contact but still makes the point. I was writing for a television special and had to contact one of the guest stars with some script changes. For whatever reason, he was surly during this taping. Everyone around the set was complaining about what a bear he'd been. I didn't relish bringing new jokes to him right before rehearsal, but I had to.

He lived up to his "notices" when I met him in his dressing room. He accepted the changes, but reluctantly, and with a sarcastic remark about each one. All I wanted to do was complete my chores and get out of there.

But no, I thought to myself. I genuinely liked the new television series he produced and starred in. It was well written and well performed and I was going to tell him that before I left, even if he bit my head off.

"I really like your new show," I said. "It's got some very creative writing and a great cast."

He held out his hand to shake mine and his demeanor changed dramatically. He dropped the wise guy act and was very friendly. "Thank you," he said. "We're very proud of it."

We talked for several minutes—as two honest-to-goodness humane, friendly people—about the writing, casting and making of his show.

Even though he was a successful, wealthy, international star, he appreciated this compliment. He enjoyed talking with a writer about the writing of his series.

So your sincere letter of praise will be noticed by a major publishing house, a well-known agent, or a best-selling author.

Keep It Professional

Many of the movers and shakers in the writing industry don't mind being contacted by other professionals. What everyone objects to, though, is having time wasted.

If I'm an agent, I'm interested in your proposal about a potential book project. However, I'm not interested in the fact that your brother-in-law recently lost his job and that your son just made the Little League All-Star team—unless you're writing about job placement or children's sports.

Avoid "cutesy" letters. They're not only annoying to read, they're difficult to interpret. When you do jokes face to face, you can smile or gesture. You can do something to let the other person know you're joking. On paper, none of that is available to you or to the reader. Consequently, the reader of the letter winds up saying, "What the hell is this person talking about?"

I recently got a letter asking for some information. The writer said, "I've always wanted to be a writer, but I'm not too smart and have no talent, so I thought I'd try comedy." Was that a put-on? An attempt at a joke? Or is this a person who honestly thinks that writing humor is reserved for lamebrained incompetents? It's hard to tell.

Stick to the Point

Keep your correspondence concise and to the point, and generally limit yourself to one point per letter. Laundry lists of requests are intimidating, and they're time-consuming to answer.

If I receive a letter asking a professional question, I might type out a quick response when I have a break in my workday. By quick, I mean one that doesn't take too much of my time, not one that I dismiss without serious thought. But if it's a letter asking fifteen questions, each demanding a reply, it will require considerable thought, time and effort. I can't write that as quickly. Consequently, I might postpone that response until it gets buried under other papers on my desk, and eventually discarded without a response.

Be Specific

If you're writing for advice, information or a favor, be specific. Ask for specific advice, information or the favor.

General questions, such as "How can I become a better

writer?" are too general for a response. They should be asked of a writing teacher rather than a professional friend.

Do Your Own Research

Professionals that you write to are neither writing schools nor researchers. Limit any questions you have for them to information that only they can give.

I receive many letters in which the correspondent wants me to do his work. "Can you give me the address of NBC?" Certainly I can, but you can also find it with a little bit of work on your own. Why should I do it for you? "Can you tell me who produces 'Murphy Brown'?" Yes I can, but you can find it just by watching the credits at the end of the show.

"Would you read the enclosed short story and perhaps suggest some endings that might make it more marketable?" No.

Write to the Right People

Professionals are often happy to help, but only when they *can* help. Be sure the person you write to can (and should) do what you ask.

I get many requests from comedy writers to read a situation-comedy script or a screenplay. This is not only a demand on my time, but it's fruitless. I can't hire the writer and I can't buy the product.

I would prefer that these people send this manuscript to the marketplace. Send it to a show or a studio. If the producers like it, they can buy it. If they don't like it, they might offer suggestions to improve it. That's their business; it's not mine.

Allow Them to Respond

A letter doesn't demand a response. There are no laws in this nation—either statutory or traditional—that require anyone to answer every letter received. People can, if they choose, ignore your communication.

"I've always liked Jane Doe's romance novels. I thought she was the greatest author in the world. So I wrote to her about my book about the Galapagos Islands, and she never even had the courtesy to respond. I'll never read any of her books again."

Don't get angry and vindictive if people decide not to answer your letters. That's their right and privilege.

The Proverbial "SASE"

If your letter, though, does encourage a response, send a self-addressed stamped envelope (SASE). It's a professional courtesy, that's all. If you're sending a complimentary letter or a thank-you message, the SASE, of course, is unnecessary. But anything that requires a return should include it.

The telephone is a more precarious method of developing new contacts. People can open and read their mail at their leisure but must answer the telephone when it rings. In that sense, it's more of an unwelcome intrusion. But it is quick, and more intimate than the mail. It is a valid and worthwhile way of meeting new friends in the industry.

Now for some thoughts on telephone courtesy.

Be Considerate

The telephone can span the globe. You can pick up a receiver in New York and talk to someone in Bangkok. You can also talk to someone in Los Angeles. Unfortunately, if you call at 9:00 A.M. in New York, you're ringing the telephone at 6:00 A.M. in Los Angeles. I know. I've received calls in the wee hours from people who then explained, "Oh, I'm sorry. I didn't realize it was so early there."

Also, people have busy hours of the day and relaxed hours when they would prefer to handle calls. If possible, find out when during the day people would rather have you call.

Do *not* pester with telephone calls. Keep them to a reasonable number and reasonably spaced.

Be Brief

Talking on the telephone is immediate, unlike a letter that can be postponed and read or reread at a more convenient time. A telephone call is now and must be dealt with immediately. Therefore, respect the professional's time and keep your calls reasonably brief and free of as much idle chitchat as possible.

Be Prepared

Have a specific purpose in mind for your call, and get to it quickly. Know what you want to say and say it concisely. Also, have within reach any documentation you might need.

Be Gracious

One advantage a telephone call has over a letter is that the exchange of information is immediate. That can also be one of the disadvantages.

More than a few times I've been asked for advice over the telephone, offered it, and then had it challenged. It's not only a blow to my ego, but it's also time-consuming to debate the value of one's counsel on the telephone.

By all means, ask any questions you have about the advice or information offered. The person who offers it surely wants it to be understood. But she may not want to justify and defend it.

Any friends you make in the writing industry have the potential to enhance your career. They are worth your effort to develop. In any exchange, though, the important elements are to be courteous and to be professional.

I once had a luncheon meeting with a television star to discuss auditioning my material to write his nightclub act. We discussed ideas only briefly over lunch. After lunch he said, "I want you to write my act."

I was pleased, but stunned. I said, "We hardly discussed

ideas, and you haven't really seen any of my material. What convinced you to make this decision?"

He said, "The way you treated our waitress."

Courtesy and professionalism — those virtues alone can help get your career moving in the right direction.

CHAPTER 27

SET A QUOTA FOR QUERIES

I attended a sales conference once and listened to a motivational speaker preach what sounded like heresy to a group of salespeople. He said, "I love to hear the word 'no.' Some of you may be frustrated, disappointed, dejected when you call on a client and he says 'no.' Not me. I'm elated, delighted, overjoyed."

Motivational speakers tend to get overdramatic, but this was ridiculous. He was hired to get these people to sell more product, to get more "yes" responses from their clients, and here he was exulting when he heard "no."

He went on to explain.

"You may be the best salesperson in the world. You may have the most efficient product in your briefcase. You may have the most polished and persuasive sales pitch rehearsed to perfection. Statistics still show that nine out of ten people you contact won't buy from you. That's not me saying that. I don't manufacture these figures. Those are the statistics that have been compiled over the years. Nine people are going to say 'no' to you before one of them says 'yes.' "

It seemed like pretty depressing statistics and a demoralizing talk coming from an alleged motivational lecturer.

"Therefore, I'm delighted when I call on a client and he gives me a negative response. Even after I try to sell him, he remains firm. His answer is 'no.' I hang up or I leave his office with joy in my heart because now I've lowered the odds. Now only eight people will say 'no' before I get one to say 'yes.' Now only eight people will refuse my product before I finally get one who will make me some money." He was beginning to make some sense. "Every 'no' you hear brings you closer to that money-making 'yes.'"

Do you see his point? He was talking pure percentages. If only one out of ten responds positively, use those statistics. If you want one sale, contact ten customers. If you want ten sales, contact a hundred customers.

Obviously, that's a mathematical oversimplification, but the message is: The more customers a salesperson calls on, the more chances she has and, most likely, the more sales she will make.

Writers are salespeople. Manuscripts and ideas are your product, and query letters are your "cold calls." As our motivational friend advised, you may have the best product in the world, and you may be a charming and persuasive person. You're still going to get your percentage of rejection notices.

So how do you lift your freelance sales another notch? Increase your queries.

Bud Gardner in 1987 was interviewed in *Round Table*, a comedy writers' newsletter I publish monthly. Bud is a professional freelance writer, winner of the 1983 Jack London Award. He also taught writing at the time of this interview at American River College in northern California.

In ten years, Bud's students had sold more than two thousand articles and almost thirty books, earning collectively almost $500,000. Since the interview, his students have pushed the total to more than $1 million in sales.

In the *Round Table* interview, Bud outlined his suggested form for a good query letter: "Open with a hook lead, followed by your theme. State why your idea is important. Name the sources or subject of your article. Get in pertinent details showing you've done your homework and talked to people. Offer pictures and maybe a bit about yourself. Ask if the editor wants to see your article. Then exit."

He then recommended a strict quota of queries. "Write and mail at least one query per day for a month, and you'll not only turn out better queries, I predict you'll have all the article go-aheads you can handle."

That's pretty definite encouragement for advancing your career — "You'll have all the article go-aheads you can handle." It's the same principle the sales motivational speaker was advancing: If you want more sales, make more contacts.

Quotas sound rigid and demanding — almost sophomoric, in a way. It's a forced discipline that a teacher might impose on a recalcitrant student, not a scheduling device for a mature, selling writer. Yet quotas offer benefits for mature, selling writers at all levels of success. Practically every article I read about noted authors tells me that they impose some sort of a quota on themselves.

"I get up and I write religiously every day from seven in the morning until three in the afternoon."

"I write at least ten pages each day before I turn off my word processor."

These types of quotas are common from authors. Many of them adhere to strict disciplines because they recognize that writers — or anyone who works for himself — absolutely require discipline. So don't dismiss a quota system simply because it sounds childish. It may be, but that child who still exists in all of us — and who incidentally probably makes us more imaginative writers — wants to avoid some work.

I recommend a quota schedule to any aspiring comedy writers I work with. In fact, I demand it. I have been known to terminate working relationships with some promising students, if they failed to write so many jokes per week. When the jokes stopped — for whatever reason — our professional relationship stopped.

I did let the students set the quota. They knew how much time they had to devote to writing and how advanced they were. No quota should be so demanding that it causes physical or emotional strain, yet neither should it be so simple that it offers no challenge. You'll hurt yourself if you try to get in shape by doing 2,500 push-ups a day, but you'll gain nothing if you set and maintain a strict regimen of one push-up a day.

I champion the quota system for several reasons.

It Is a Discipline

It's not a statute; it's not a contract. You are free to deviate from it anytime you want. But it's there. It's a reminder that you have work to get done and if you don't do it, if you fall behind, it's your fault. You have no one to blame but yourself.

It's easy for us to concentrate on one particular project and shelve the others. Sometimes we push them so far back on the shelf that they're either forgotten or abandoned as hopeless.

A quota keeps them present in our minds. It's the tiny speck of sand that irritates the oyster. And in trying to relieve the irritation, we writers, like the mollusk, eventually build a gem: our body of creative work.

It Stimulates Ideas

Good ideas are precious. If one suddenly visits us, no matter where we are, we try to jot it down. I know you've written premises on cocktail napkins. You've probably jotted down concepts on whatever scratch paper was by your bed in the middle of the night and tried to translate it the next morning. We've all done it. Commit this idea to paper; don't let it get away.

Many ideas get away from us because we don't bother to pursue them in the first place. Fishers always tell the tale of the big one that got away. Well, hundreds of fish have escaped my hook because I don't own a rod, a reel or a hook. I simply don't go fishing.

A quota like the one Bud Gardner suggests forces you to go fishing for ideas every day. You have to catch at least one. Some of them might be too small to keep. Some of them might be average. One of them, though, might be the biggie. You wouldn't catch it unless you forced yourself to fish every day.

It's Gradual and Painless

Consider the body of your writing output. It's extensive. So extensive, probably, that if asked to do it again, you wouldn't have the time.

I have twenty-eight volumes of original jokes on my shelf right now. They represent only one client. There are about 3,300 monologues in them, which represent probably 100,000 gags. When I think about it in bulk, it astounds me. If you had asked me twenty years ago if I would ever have written that much material, I'd say, "No way."

But it's there. It exists because it was done over the years, on demand. I wrote what had to be written, and it grew to that amount.

A quota system, even for queries, can do the same. It can build to a body of sales that is formidable. Bud Gardner's college students have generated seven-figure sales. That's incredible, but they built that amount because they sent out the queries. They called on lots of customers and made lots of sales.

It Keeps Your Marketing Active

The quota system keeps your marketing flowing, keeps your name and product before the buyers. It's continuous, relentless. It's much easier than a stop-and-start system in which you must keep overcoming your own inertia.

If you've ever had a car stuck in the snow, you know what I mean. You push that vehicle to get it going. You rock it back and forth while you give it gas to get it out of that rut. Once you get that baby out, you don't want to stop again until it's safely parked in your own driveway. You know that once you stop those wheels from turning, there's a chance you may have to go through the turmoil all over again.

The quota system keeps your marketing moving.

As the publisher of *Round Table*, I decided in 1987, one month after Bud Gardner's interview appeared, to try his recommendation. I wasn't a magazine writer then; I was a television writer working long hours on a weekly series. As an experiment for the other readers, though, I accepted Bud's challenge.

I developed one premise, researched a potential market, and mailed out one query letter for each working day of the month. That totaled twenty letters to various publications.

I sold seven of the articles. That's not a bad percentage. And this was only a first mailing. I didn't continue the experiment, but the queries that were returned could have been submitted to other markets and might have sold on their second, third or fourth submissions. That would raise the percentages dramatically.

Many of the editors who bought these first submissions also asked for second pieces.

To me, this was dramatic proof that you can make things happen and increase sales by increasing your requests for sales. As the sales motivator said, "The more 'no's' you get, the more 'yes's' you'll get, too."

Bud Gardner recommended one query per day. You're certainly professional and mature enough to tailor that number to fit your desires. If you want to get your sales and career shifted to a higher gear, send out more and more query letters on a regular, continuing basis.

CHAPTER 28

THE SCATTER-GUN APPROACH

There's a story about an old minister who is desperately in need of money to fund his ministry, but the man has unflinching faith. He doesn't worry about his debts; he simply prays for money. He says, "Lord, let me hit the lottery," and goes serenely to sleep.

He doesn't win any money, though.

He prays again, just as sincerely and just as determined that his prayers will be answered. "Lord, let me hit the lottery."

Nothing happens.

This continues for some time and the old man begins to be offended by God's apparent callousness. But he continues to pray to hit the lottery.

He never does.

Finally, one night the Lord appears to him. The minister speaks his mind. He says, "I don't know if I should even talk to You. I've prayed faithfully for Your help. I asked You to provide funds for my church by letting me hit the lottery, but You never did."

The Lord said, "Reverend, do me a favor, will you? Buy a ticket."

All writers know that to make a sale, you have to enter the marketplace. You have to buy the ticket. And if you want to move your career to the next plateau, you might have to invest in several tickets.

I grew up in the city, South Philadelphia. I had to do my

share of street fighting. Back then, it was more ritualistic than vicious. The loser might wind up with a bruised lip or a bloody nose, nothing more serious. However, since I was a small kid, I was generally the loser.

Once, though, I was challenged by a kid even smaller than me. I was delighted. Finally, a challenger I could overpower.

"Let me at him," I yelled. "Hold my coat."

I was eager to get this altercation under way. I needed a win badly to bolster my young manhood.

Our friends defined the rules and widened out into a circle for us two combatants. When the start signal was given, this tiny dynamo rushed at me like a maniacal windmill. He came at me head down, swinging both arms in circular motions.

I couldn't block all of his punches and I didn't have time to throw any of my own. I couldn't grab him and wrestle him to the ground because he never stayed still. He'd just retreat and charge again with those devastating, unceasing bolo punches.

I took a beating that day. Oh, I had the obligatory bruised lip and bloody nose, but the emotional defeat was the more telling. I couldn't even whip someone smaller than me.

He defeated me with quantity. My buddies and I in our retreat agreed that I was the superior fighter. He simply won because he threw 3,997 punches and landed twelve, while I threw absolutely no punches and landed none of them.

He used the scatter-gun approach. He had fists flying at me from every direction and with never-ending frequency. Sooner or later, one of them had to flatten my nose.

That little guy raised his fighting reputation another notch that day, and you can use the same style to lift your writing career.

Come at editors and publishers with queries, proposals and manuscripts flying. Bombard them with product. Razzle-dazzle them with quantity. Sooner or later you'll get someone's attention, just like my opponent got mine with a pop to the proboscis.

By the scatter-gun approach, I don't mean sending multiple submissions or even multiple queries. It's a step beyond that. If you have an idea for a book, it's fine to send query letters to a dozen publishers to see which asks to see a manuscript or proposal. That's standard operating procedure.

Scatter-gunning, though, is not sending one proposal to several potential buyers; it's sending several different proposals to various potential buyers.

For example, if you're a rock climber, you might propose a how-to book on climbing, a children's book explaining the hobby of climbing, a reference book on climbing equipment, a history of climbing, a reference book listing the best places for climbing, climbing for beginners, and countless more. These could all go to different types of publishers, and you'd have bettered your chances of having one of these houses agree to publish one or more of your books.

If you want to create a television series, do several different premises, write them up as treatments, and send them to various producers, networks or agents.

You're not only buying many lottery tickets, but you're buying them from many different lotteries.

Scatter-gunning is dissecting a basic idea, extracting other ideas that are contained within it, and exploring tangential or related items. You see this principle in operation constantly. Bicycle shops sell bicycles, right? They also sell baskets to put on the front of bikes, children's seats to put on the back, water bottles, and racks to hold water bottles. They sell cycling clothes and shoes. They sell pumps for your tires and tools so you can repair your own bike. They even sell books that suggest interesting places to ride your bike, and they sell decals that say you've been to those places—whether you've been there or not.

Charles Schulz, the artist who created "Peanuts," makes millions from the sale of stationery, clothing, toys and various other products featuring the Peanuts characters. Disney, Matt Groening (the creator of "The Simpsons") and many others do the same thing.

Major corporations expand like this all the time. The products they sell create markets for other related products.

The scatter-gun approach also applies to your markets. One idea, with some ingenuity, might apply to several markets. For example, suppose you want to write a cookbook. You would gather your recipes, write your outline, search out appropriate publishers who buy cookbooks in your market list, and mail out queries or proposals.

If you're successful, you'll publish a book, and cooks all over the country will buy it.

But what about publishers who don't publish cookbooks? Can you sell to them? A juvenile publisher might be interested in a first cookbook for children. You might collect some good camping recipes and sell them to a publisher of outdoor books. How about offering a satire on cookbooks to a humor publisher? A series of celebrity recipes, accompanied with a profile of the celebs, might sell to any of several magazines.

You get the idea. Buy more tickets to more lotteries, and you have a better chance of winning.

The scatter-gun principle, like the previous chapter on a quota for queries, is pure mathematics. The more ideas you circulate, the better your chances of selling. But that's not the only benefit the scatter-gun approach has for giving your career a boost.

It Opens New Avenues

Scatter-gunning, by definition, forces you into new writing arenas. You never know which of those might become your central focus. I know a television comedy writer who accepted an assignment on a children's animated show almost as a joke. "Just once I'd like to write for a pen-and-ink drawing who can't throw the script to the floor and complain about the lousy writing," was his incentive.

He enjoyed the writing and stayed with it. He's now among the top-paid and most highly respected animation writers in Hollywood.

You just never know.

It Forces You to Expand Your Creativity

The one criticism I have of beginning comedy writers is this: You stop too soon. Most beginners stop too early on both the individual jokes and on the premise. They jot down a funny joke and consider it finished. It usually isn't. The phrasing has to be explored, polished, perfected. The idea is there, but it has to be expressed as a better joke.

Then they write four or five jokes on one idea and consider it exhausted. It isn't. There are other angles to take on that same premise, other comedic areas to be mined.

I tell beginning writers to do at least thirty jokes on a topic. It's demanding and, at times, seems impossible. Those who stay with it, though, usually find that their best writing comes after that initial surge. They think they're finished, they persevere through the dry period, then they come up with innovative ideas.

That's what this process will help other writers do: persevere. Think about a project beyond the initial inspiration. Force, if you will, further creativity out of yourself. You'll discover that it's not only good for the premise, it's good for your career.

CHAPTER 29

FOCUS YOUR ENERGY

I once heard an athlete make a statement that confused me. He was a shot-putter who said that his longest toss was always his easiest. "Wait a minute," I said to myself. "How could the longest be the easiest? It would have to take more exertion, more effort, more pain." But he explained that when everything worked together, the timing was right, and it was actually easier to toss the shot further. It made sense.

One time I foolishly signed on for a golf vacation with some pretty good golfers. Two of my companions had golf handicaps under five — pretty good golfers. The other man was a question mark, but he was a fairly good athlete, so I assumed he would be a better-than-average golfer. I was a duffer, a raw beginner.

So I practiced. I took a few lessons and went to the driving range regularly. I got to where I could hit a decent shot off the tee. In fact, I felt pretty proud of myself, almost cocky.

When we finally got to our vacation spot and out to the first tee, I was determined to make a surprising showing. I teed the ball up and took a few practice swings. I knew I could knock the ball a good ways down the middle of the fairway, but suddenly that wasn't enough. I wanted to dazzle my companions with an astounding shot, one they would talk about for the remaining eighteen holes. So I swung a little harder. Actually, I swung a lot harder. The ball went four feet.

Honest to goodness, it went four feet. No one laughed. No

one said anything. I just picked the ball up, put it back on the tee, swung again, and hit a decent shot. And play continued.

But what happened to that first shot? If I could hit the ball fairly consistently and well, and I swung harder, shouldn't the ball go farther? Obviously not. Why?

Because to hit a golf ball well, the club must hit the ball in the right spot, it must be going in the right direction, and all of the power must be concentrated on that moment of impact. My extra exertion on the swing threw all that off. Yes, I hit the ball harder, but not on the sweet spot. I hit the top of the ball. Instead of propelling the ball down the fairway, I drove it into the ground. It bounced up and landed four feet away. All of my club energy was going in the wrong direction.

That can sometimes happen with our writing careers, too. We can waste a lot of energy going in the wrong direction. It happened to me.

Early in my writing career, I was scrambling to make things happen. I had contracts and agreements all over the city. I'd make ten bucks a week here, fifteen bucks a week there, and so on. I'd write for any comedian and any disc jockey who would have me. It was a lot of work and I was turning out quite a bit of product, but I didn't seem to be getting anywhere. "Spinning my wheels" was an appropriate description of my writing career then.

I took time out to think about it. I terminated all of my comedy-writing agreements except for the two most promising. My work improved and my fortunes did, also. Within one year I was where I wanted to be: writing comedy on national television.

With the multiple contracts, I did mediocre work for many people and earned mediocre pay. Mediocrity is never enough to project your career ahead. It's usually just enough to keep you where you are.

By narrowing my work down to the two most promising contracts, I focused my energy and improved both the quality and quantity of my work for those clients. It worked. It got me and my talents noticed. It moved me up to the next plateau.

To review your output with an eye to focusing your energy,

switch hats for awhile. Forgo the artist in your soul and become the businessperson. As someone wise in the ways of the entrepreneurial world once said, "If you can't measure it, you can't manage it." Take some time to measure your work. Analyze it. Review it. See exactly what you get for the work you do.

They do this in the business world all the time. They look at the work each employee does and how much that employee gets paid, then decide whether that person merits a modest raise or an immodest "chewing out." You should do that periodically with yourself. Evaluate your own performance and refine it. Make it as efficient as the shot-putter's championship throw.

ANALYZE YOUR WORK SCHEDULE

Create a log of all your writing projects and the time devoted to each. We get so involved in our projects that we often don't know how much time and effort we give to each. But as good businesspeople we should know, and remember, that writing is a business, too.

With this record you'll know better how much time you devote to each of your projects and the various facets of your writing career.

ANALYZE THE COMPENSATION FOR YOUR WORK

Businesspeople speak of, and complain of, the "80-20" factor. They theorize that people devote 80 percent of their work time to clients who account for only 20 percent of their profit. I don't know how mathematically correct the theory is, but the idea is that workers often devote an inordinate percentage of their time to those contracts that deliver a small monetary gain.

You can test the theory in your own business by checking your records. Now that you have a listing of how much time you devote to each facet of your writing career, record also how much you receive financially in return for each. With a few pushes of some buttons on your pocket calculator, come up with a dollars-per-hour figure for each item on your list. You'll know exactly which of your efforts are the most efficient.

Some of these figures may astound you, and should definitely give you some direction as to which writing avenues to pursue with more vigor. For example, if writing humorous magazine articles pays at an hourly rate of ten times what writing humorous greeting cards pays, perhaps you should abandon the greeting-card writing and concentrate on the article writing.

I'll leave that sort of decision making to each individual writer, but this report you've just generated will give you a clear picture of the financial status of your writing business.

CONSIDER POTENTIAL INCOME

Unfortunately, not all rewards can be measured on a dollars-per-hour basis. One youngster can graduate from high school and immediately take a job somewhere for, oh, say, five dollars an hour. Another youngster graduates from high school and registers for college at a cost of, oh, say, twenty thousand dollars a year. One has a positive dollar-per-hour income, the other has a negative income. In the long run, however, the negative income will be more productive. You have to consider the potential long-term effect.

That should be a column that you add to your business analysis, also. What is the potential payoff? You might want to consider some of your lower dollar-per-hour assignments simply because they have greater potential. Or some of your present high-paying jobs may be keeping you from exploring the better-looking long-term contracts.

Not all work you do at your writing desk is necessarily for an immediate monetary reward. Some of it is an investment in yourself. Make that part of the equation.

Put a column for potential income into your analysis sheet.

CONSIDER YOUR PERSONAL ENJOYMENT

Until now, the study has been about income. Woody Allen said, "Money is better than poverty, if only for financial reasons." I suppose it is, but we writers don't always do things for financial rewards. Artists reserve the right to be naive — sometimes stupid — about monetary matters, for the sake of our art. We march to the beat of a different drummer.

Nevertheless, it's good to know which beat you're marching to. Make a note of this, too, in your work schedule review. Next to each item add a column for a rating of how much you enjoy each project. Give it an absolute zero if you can't stand turning the word processor on and beginning a certain hated assignment. Give it a five if you don't really dislike this project, but there are other things you'd rather work on. Give it a ten if you can't wait to get at it.

You get the idea. You can devise your own rating system, maybe a simple " + " or " − ", or a "yes" or "no" in this column; but indicate somehow whether you enjoy working on this project or not. It'll help you get a clearer picture of how you spend your writing time now and how you might alter it to improve it.

ASK, "IS IT FURTHERING MY CAREER?"

Another column — an important one — to add to your checklist: "Is this project helping me get where I want to go?" That's it — yes or no. Is this work you're doing making you a better writer? Is it making you a more marketable writer? Is it helping you progress toward your goal?

You've now generated a full report that tells you how much time you devote to each project, how much you earn from that project, how much that amounts to in an hourly rate, what the potential income of each project is, how much you enjoy each project, and whether it is helping you attain your goal or not. You have a pretty fair basis to make some decisions. Now you have to decide what decisions you want to make.

There are three points of view to use now in drawing conclusions from this report. I'll call them:

1. The Samuel Johnson point of view
2. The Dean Martin point of view
3. The Calvin Coolidge point of view

The Samuel Johnson Point of View

If you believe, as Samuel Johnson did, that "no man but a block-head ever wrote except for money"; if gathering immediate income is your top priority (and there's nothing wrong with that); this list should be fairly simple to analyze. Keep those activities that generate the most income, the most dollars per hour. Promote more of those types of writing assignments, and eliminate those that don't pay nearly as well.

Try to make your writing operation more efficient. Focus your time and energies into those projects that have the biggest payoffs.

The Dean Martin Point of View

Dean used to say that golf was his profession. Singing was just a way for him to make money to pay the greens fees.

Mr. Martin was kidding, I think, but his premise is valid. There is a way for writers to balance their efforts so that part of their work pays the bills for the other part—the part that may be more enjoyable, but less profitable at the moment.

Your report should help you decide how much of your workday to devote to the pragmatic part of writing, the paying-the-bills part. It will show you which of those projects is most productive, most profitable. It can also show you which profitable activities have the most potential to develop your career.

And it will show you how much time you have left, after paying your expenses, to devote to pure speculation, pure investment in your writing future.

The Calvin Coolidge Point of View

President Coolidge said, "Nothing in the world can take the place of persistence. Talent will not; nothing is more common than unsuccessful men with talent. Genius will not; unrewarded genius is almost a proverb. Education alone will not; the world is full of educated derelicts. Persistence and determination alone are omnipotent."

Some writers don't need income now. They just want to write with all of their mind and soul focused on the future, on their career. Bless them.

Some writers don't care about bills or expenses. They keep their mind and soul focused on the future, too, and believe that the present will take care of itself somehow. Bless them, too.

If that's your philosophy, this report will also point out which activities for you to proceed with. It will clarify where your energies should be focused.

Remember, that's the purpose of this business report as well as this entire chapter: to focus your energy. All of us want something, and we can more easily attain it if we focus our energy on that goal. We may differ in what we want and how we go about getting it, but we still have to focus. As the shot-putter in the opening of this chapter advised, it's the easiest way to do it.

One other note on focusing your energy before leaving this chapter: If you have a goal as a writer, pursue that goal. Go at it headlong and with abandon. Go for what you want. Many writers I've worked with go for something else with the hopes of "trading that in" for what they want.

Let me give you an example. Some comedy writers want to write situation comedies for television. That's a worthwhile goal. So they say, "I'll write jokes for comedians for awhile, and then I'll start writing situation comedies." Or they even say, "I'll become an actor, and then when I get a few roles, I can begin writing some of the scripts."

Both approaches are wrong if the goal is to become a situation-comedy writer. If this person wants to get some experience as a joke writer or a performer to educate himself to be a better situation-comedy writer, that's all right; but it's not a back-door method to achieving the original goal.

And the same applies to other writers. "I want to write

poetry, so I'll sell some travel articles to magazines first." "I want to write mainstream novels, so I'll begin by writing a few children's novels first." And so on.

This approach is wrong for at least two reasons. First, it can be counterproductive because, as I've said before, people in the arts tend to pigeonhole your talents. If you're a children's novelist, you're a children's novelist. In the industry's mind, you don't necessarily have what it takes to be a mainstream author. In television, if you're a joke writer, you're not a situation-comedy writer. Conversely, if you're a situation-comedy writer, you're not a joke writer.

The thinking may be erroneous, but it exists. So even if you get the success you want in the first field, it doesn't mean that you can automatically shuttle over to the other. In fact, it may be harder to make the transition.

Second, this idea of sneaking in the back door implies that one profession or genre is easier than the other. None is; they're simply different from one another. Writing juvenile novels doesn't require less dedication or skill than writing genre or mainstream novels. Writing jokes for a comedian is no easier than writing teleplays. Writing articles is no less trouble than writing good poetry. They're all different.

So, since it takes just as much effort to go into one area as another, why not devote your energy into the field that you really want?

Focus on that, and get your career moving in that direction.

CHAPTER 30

TAKE *a* CHANCE *on* YOURSELF

I heard a story some time ago about a diminutive, feisty college football coach who was berating one of his mammoth linemen. His tirade, with only the acceptable words left in, went something like: "You're a big, lazy, dumb galoot. You've got no fight in you, no spirit, no heart, no gumption. You know what you are? You're chicken. No, you're worse than chicken. You're a chicken who loafs on the football field, that's what you are. You let the other guys push you around. You let guys who are only half your size walk all over you. They don't weigh nearly as much as you do and they're pushing you all over the field. You're a bum, is what you are, a lazy bum. You gotta get some fight into you, man. You gotta get some fight. Why, if I was your size I would have been heavyweight champion of the world. *Are there any questions?*"

The big lineman said, "Just one, Coach. What kept you from becoming the flyweight champion of the world?"

The kid had a point. Very few excuses for lack of accomplishment hold up under close scrutiny. They're usually rationalizations that blame fate, circumstances, timing, or something or someone else for our misfortune. The fault, though, as Shakespeare eloquently said, lies not in the stars, but in ourselves.

But let's put a positive, rather than a negative, spin on this idea. We have the power within ourselves to achieve what we want to achieve. As *Think and Grow Rich* author Napoleon Hill said, "Whatever the mind of man can conceive and believe, it can achieve."

I've mentioned before that my television agent always told me, "Get to work. You've got a government grant." Television work is frantic; the deadlines are inflexible. The work, good or bad, has to be done by Friday, that's all there is to it. It's often exhausting and stressful work. Vacations are welcomed.

But that's the good side of the coin: There is plenty of time off in television. Many shows work three weeks and take the fourth week off. There is a hiatus at the end of each season. There are also times when a show is canceled, and you don't have to report to work even though you continue to get paid.

My agent wanted some work out of me during those down periods. He'd want a spec screenplay, some ideas for a series, something. "You've got a government grant." What he was saying was, "Invest in yourself. Do some work on speculation that I can sell."

That's also what this chapter suggests to you: Invest in yourself.

Most of you are reading this book because you're somewhat dissatisfied with the progress of your career. Why else would you buy a book that tells you how to shift your career into high gear? If you're even slightly dissatisfied, it's because there's some writing that you want to do but haven't yet done. Now this book is advising you to do it. As the Nike ads say, "Just do it."

Do you want to write a television situation comedy? Do it. Do you want to write a screenplay? Do it. How about a novel? Same advice. A nonfiction book, a children's book, a book of poetry? Whatever it is you want to do, do it. Take a chance on yourself.

That "take a chance" phrase is the fly in the ointment. That's the little hint of risk that might stop some of us. We're afraid of what it might cost. Ironically, though, we usually put higher price tags on things than they deserve.

When I was offered a chance to come to Hollywood to write for television it was a frightening proposition — to uproot an entire family, move from one coast to another, leave a job in which

I'd invested thirteen years, and begin a new career in something that I wasn't at all familiar with. Yet when I analyzed all the risks, it amounted to taking a chance on a potentially high-paying career and if I failed, all it would have cost me was my two weeks' vacation for the next year. I would have lost no money, I could have gotten my job back because my company promised to hold it for me, and our family would have had a cross-country adventure. The fears were unfounded. They usually are.

Here's a four-step proposal that will help you take a chance on yourself.

1. Decide what you *really* want to do.
2. Find out as much as you can about it.
3. Budget the time and money to try it.
4. Do it.

DECIDE WHAT YOU *REALLY* WANT TO DO

Be honest with yourself. Don't pretend you really want to do what the world says you should do. Honestly confess to yourself that you want to do *this*, whether "this" is wise or foolish, profitable or costly, acceptable or bizarre, high-brow or low.

And be bold. Admit that you really want to do something even if everyone else you know advises against it, or even rejects you because of it. This is your dream, not theirs.

FIND OUT AS MUCH AS YOU CAN ABOUT IT

Unfortunately, we don't always want to do things we know about. On the plus side, though, there is nothing in this world that we can't learn. If you want to write a movie, there are books in the library or bookstore that can tell you how to write screenplays and in what form to submit screenplays. There are books about everything.

There are also people you can contact to ask.

So begin doing some research. Find out who else has succeeded at the type of writing you want to explore. Read and learn how they did it.

Find out who buys this type of writing. Subscribe to magazines that tell you about this particular field. Read the articles and study the ads. The ads will lead you to other avenues of research. It's a never-ending chain of information.

BUDGET THE TIME AND MONEY TO TRY IT

Money and time are recurring problems, but they needn't become insurmountable obstacles. Not if you budget and plan.

I was producing a television series when I contracted to write my first book. As I mentioned, television deadlines are unyielding, and the production day generally lasts longer than eight hours. I didn't think I had enough time to write a book.

However, I devoted some time to planning because I wanted to do a book. I realized I had two hours a day of driving time on the freeways. With some foresight, I could use that time.

Each morning, I planned which topic I would work on for the book. On the way to and from work, I dictated random thoughts and notes into a voice-activated recorder. It didn't take my hands off the wheel and it didn't distract me from my driving. I was merely conversing with my readers while I drove.

I paid a typist to transcribe my notes daily. Then on the weekend, I converted those extensive notes into chapters of the book, one chapter written on Saturday, the other on Sunday. In four months' time, with little or no invasion of my television-producing duties, I had completed the first draft of my first book.

Money is even easier to budget because there's more of it around than there is time. We all have only twenty-four hours a day to manipulate, but we can always earn more money somewhere. Or we can borrow from Peter to pay Paul until we finish our book. The advance then will be enough to pay Peter back and also earn Paul a little profit, too.

DO IT

This is the easy part. Just do it. Do it on spec if you have to. Plan it, begin it, and don't stop until it's done.

Then sell it.

Even if you don't sell it, you've gained, because having successfully completed one project like this, you gain confidence in your next one. You also gain knowledge. Each time you write, you learn something. You get better at it.

Even if the world calls this first endeavor a failure, it might be the key to your success. Your next book may sell. Your next screenplay may be a box-office smash. Your next book of poems may get critical raves.

Take a chance on yourself. The dividends are usually worth the investment.

PART IV

LOOK TO YOUR YOURSELF – AGAIN

"I know of no more encouraging fact than the unquestionable ability of man to elevate his life by a conscious endeavor."

HENRY DAVID THOREAU

CHAPTER 31

PARTING WORDS

In these last few sentences I'd like to refer you to chapter one. That's the kind of book this is intended to be: not one you read and discard, but one you reread and refer to periodically.

Your career has already outgrown some of the suggestions in this book; others you may find use for in the future.

I won't suggest that you reread chapter one because I know whenever I see that recommendation in a book, I ignore it. Do recall, though, in general terms its message: It's your career.

There's an oft-told tale that I'd like to recount one more time before it's irretrievably lost to cliché-land. It's about a youngster who wanted to confound a certain wise man. He captured a butterfly and held it in his closed hands. He said to the wise man: "I have something here. In your wisdom tell me if it is alive or dead."

The sage knew that if he said the creature was alive, the lad would crush it before opening his hands. If he said it was dead, the youth would open his hands and let it flutter away.

The wise man said, "The answer is in your hands."

Chapter one reminds you that this is your writing career. The answer is in your hands.

INDEX

and writing quotas, 128-129
Dialogue, 103
Diller, Phyllis, 2, 28, 37, 170-171, 194
Discipline, 9, 51-52, 206
and quotas, 207
Diversification, 211-214

Editing, 163-164
Editorial contacts, 189
Editors, 9, 19, 38, 160-161, 191-193
and advice, 96
versus writers, 96
Education, 18, 89-98, 225-226
and advice, 113-114
from experience, 140
from tapes, 145
teaching as, 115
writing as, 122
Evaluating
advice, 66-67
complaints, 19-20
writing, 44-45, 108, 109

Faults, correcting, 86, 88
Follow-up, 38-40, 192-193
Fraud, 31
Freelance writing, 18, 144, 164
Fundamentals, 32-33

Genre writing, 221-222
Gershwin, George, 133
Goals, 34-36, 92-93, 216-217, 221-222
achieving, 6-8, 11
choosing, 6-7, 19, 20, 225-226
realistic, 15-16
for writing quotas, 125-126

Hill, Napoleon, 223-224
Hope, Bob, 84, 125, 139, 167-168

Ideas
developing, 82-83
generating, 41, 82-83
from quotas, 207

Image, 52-53, 162-163. *See also* Professionalism
Income
attitude toward, 220-221
potential, 218
Insecurity, 63-64
Inspiration, 21-22
and reading, 23-24
Instant gratification, 11-12

Leads, 33, 50
Lecturing, 121-122, 196
Length, of written work, 163-164

Manuscript, 52-53, 158-160
Markets, new, 174
Marketing, 8, 9, 74-75, 195-197
and diversification, 212-214
and quotas, 208-209
and rejections, 204-205
scatter-gun, 210-212
Multiple submissions, 211-212

Name recognition, 175-176, 189-190
and repeat sales, 191-192
Negative people, 67-68
Networking, 176, 189, 194, 197, 202-203
Novelist, 31, 50
Novice writers, 16, 73-74, 82-84
and advice, 146
and selling, 173-174, 188
and teaching, 119-120
and television, 37-38

Office help, 164-165
On-spec writing, 112, 168-170
Organizations, 97, 98, 196
and teaching opportunities, 120-121
Outlines, 13-14, 32, 79-80
and selling, 188-189

Pace, 56-57
Pay, 14-15, 217-218
Predictability, 150-153
Preparation, 69-70, 87-88